EX

DISCARD

Other Books by SUSY SMITH

THE MEDIUMSHIP OF MRS. LEONARD
THE ENIGMA OF OUT-OF-BODY TRAVEL
ESP FOR THE MILLIONS
A SUPERNATURAL PRIMER FOR THE MILLIONS
HAUNTED HOUSES FOR THE MILLIONS
OUT-OF-BODY EXPERIENCES FOR THE MILLIONS
REINCARNATION FOR THE MILLIONS
MORE ESP FOR THE MILLIONS
WORLD OF THE STRANGE
ESP
ADVENTURES IN THE SUPERNORMAL
WIDESPREAD PSYCHIC WONDERS
SUSY SMITH'S SUPERNATURAL WORLD
TODAY'S WITCHES
PROMINENT AMERICAN GHOSTS
GHOSTS AROUND THE HOUSE
CONFESSIONS OF A PSYCHIC
ESP AND YOU
HOW TO DEVELOP YOUR ESP
SHE TALKED TO THE DEAD

*ESP and
Hypnosis*

ESP AND HYPNOSIS

SUSY SMITH

THE MACMILLAN COMPANY

NEW YORK, NEW YORK

Dedicated to MARTIN EBON
For His Friendship and For
His Ever Gracious Assistance
Especially with This Book

The Macmillan Company
866 Third Avenue, New York, N.Y. 10022
Collier-Macmillan Canada Ltd., Toronto, Ontario

Library of Congress Catalog Card Number:
72-90990

First Printing 1973

Printed in the United States of America

"Roads to Greater Reality," by Eileen J. Garrett, from *Tomorrow*, Autumn 1958, is used with the permission of the Parapsychology Foundation, Inc.

"Hypnosis: The Key to Unlocking Latent Psi Faculties," by Lee Edwards Levinson, from *International Journal of Parapsychology*, Summer 1968, is used with the permission of the author and the Parapsychology Foundation, Inc.

Thanks, too, to Veryl Smith, for her contribution.

Contents

x · Contents

1. Image of a Harlot

"HYPNOSIS IS LIKE the proverbial woman of the streets . . . every so often she becomes respectable, but soon relapses into her old status." Dr. Robert W. Lindner said that, quoting a rather saucy old teacher of whom he knew. In his Introduction to Dr. Bernard C. Gindes' book *New Concepts of Hypnosis,* Lindner added, "We are now, it seems, in the midst of one of the periods when this therapeutic coquette has put away her lace panties and rouge. And while it may be regretted by a few that her allure has suffered somewhat from this, most of us hope fervently that she continues to walk with the virtuous and to shun forever those dark alleys and narrow streets where, until lately, she has plied a trade that barely kept her alive."

Thinking of her as a tantalizing flirt instead of a prostitute, we find that most practitioners today, "in a valiant effort to insure the rehabilitation of hypnosis," are trying very hard to ignore all the back alleys and narrow streets in which she formerly traveled, to the point of almost overlooking them entirely or pretending they never existed. And yet diligent research reveals that in days past, the naughty lady, much more fascinating than most people think, produced startling evidence of extrasensory phenomena . . . and that she is still carrying on a bit here and there, now and again.

That hypnosis is today becoming popular, no one can deny. A glance at newspapers and magazines reveals this constantly. "How Hypnotism Saved Me" headlined a *Photoplay* article in September 1962, in which actor Tony Curtis told how he overcame his fear of flying so that he could make quick trips to visit his girlfriend in Germany.

Wrestling World, October 1967, explained how professional wrestler Bill Miller gained strength to "stack up" his opponents: "Hypnosis has helped me control my temper—the crowds no longer bother me." And Metropolitan Opera star Giorgio Tozzi told the *New York Post*, Saturday, November 9, 1968, that he keeps himself in top singing form by self-hypnosis.

An Associated Press story on June 20, 1969, described how Miss Mary A. Dunphy of the Philadelphia suburb of Ridley Park had her uterus removed in an operation without anesthetics. "I was never in pain," Miss Dunphy said, revealing that she had relied altogether on self-induced hypnosis during the forty-five-minute operation.

As well as reading about it, we frequently see hypnotic acts in night clubs. Oh, we know it's around, all right. But is it legitimate? Yes, by an official act of the American Medical Association, which approved its use by qualified personnel in 1958. It has since been increasingly recognized medically as an excellent substitute for some types of anesthesia and as an adjunct to psychotherapy.

What is this strange force or experience or tool we call hypnosis that apparently has so many uses? Nobody really knows, even those who proclaim it loudest. It is one of those things we define and utilize but do not explain—like electricity. It will never be really comprehended until we know a lot more than we do now about the human mind and how it works. There are as many definitions of it as there are people attempting to understand it, and few of them agree.

The dictionary says it is "a means of inducing artificially a condition akin to sleep or trance, wherein the subject is particularly susceptible to external suggestion, usually by another person called a hypnotist." The dictionary, like the doctors who are afraid the harlot will revert to her former bad habits, ignores the fact that hypnosis is also a method par excellence for bringing into play those obscure faculties of the mind known as extrasensory—telepathy (mind reading), clairvoyance (supernormal knowledge of facts or events), and prevision of the future.

The Encyclopedia of the Occult, less prejudiced against the unknown, describes hypnosis as

a peculiar state of cerebral dissociation distinguished by certain marked symptoms, the most prominent and invariable of which is a highly-increased suggestibility in the subject. The hypnotic state may be induced in a large percentage of normal individuals, or may occur spontaneously. It is recognized as having an affinity with normal sleep, and likewise with a variety of abnormal conditions, among which may be mentioned somnambulism, ecstasy, and the trances of Hindu fakirs and savage medicine men. In fact, in one or another of their forms, hypnosis and its kindred have been known in practically all countries and all times.

Hypnosis is no longer classed with the occult sciences. It has gained, though only within comparatively recent years, a definite scientific status, and no mean place in legitimate medicine. Nevertheless its history is inextricably interwoven with occultism, and even today much hypnotic phenomena is classed as "spiritualistic"; so that the consideration of hypnotism . . . is very necessary to a proper understanding of much of the occult science of our own and former times.

Although it may have "an affinity" with sleep, it is a misconception that hypnosis is a kind of sleep. "This belief," says Simeon Edmunds in *Hypnotism and E.S.P.*

no doubt arose from the facts that suggestions of sleep are often used in the induction of hypnosis, that normal sleep can sometimes be changed into hypnosis, that a hypnotized person if left undisturbed will drift into natural sleep, and that certain stages of the hypnotic trance bear a superficial resemblance to normal sleep. Braid, who coined the words "hypnosis" and "hypnotism," did so in the mistaken belief that hypnosis was a form of sleep. He later discovered his error but by then the terms, which are derived from the Greek word for sleep, had become too firmly established to change.

A moment's reflection will make it obvious that this difference is a wide one. A sleeping person is unconscious of his surroundings and will not respond if addressed, whereas the hypnotic subject will react to every suggestion and carry out highly complicated actions. Medical and scientific tests also show the dissimilarity of the two states. Reflexes are usually the same during hypnosis as in the normal waking state, but are considerably lessened during sleep. The electrical resistance of the body when asleep is up to ten times as high as when awake, but is no higher in hypnosis. The two conditions do, however, appear to meet in the case of somnambulism, or sleep-walking, in which the hypnotic state occurs spontaneously.

The medical editor of *Look* said in 1958: "Hypnosis is

neither trickery nor magic. It is a science of human behavior based on well established principles of psychology and physiology." And Dr. Milton V. Kline, one of the outstanding modern American figures in hypnosis practice and research, says that its usefulness and value "as a means of understanding and dealing with human behavior are as infinite as the capacities of the human mind, of which it is a function." Certainly, a number of experiments tend to show that it enhances recall of meaningful material to a significant degree.

Hypnosis is an effective therapeutic technique that often succeeds when other efforts fail. It is estimated that one in five Americans is able to enter a trance easily enough and deeply enough to be of use in relieving their pain. It is of great help in taking a splinter from a child or in changing dressings or in allowing a patient more easily to endure the passage of a nasal tube.

In June 1958 at the annual meeting of the American Medical Association in San Francisco, Dr. Milton J. Marmer of the University of California reported his successful use of hypnosis as the sole anesthetic in heart surgery on two teenage children. Hypnosis was actually preferred in these cases of major surgery in order to avoid the depressant effects of anesthetic drugs and to attempt to eliminate unconsciousness while the patient was on the heart-lung machine. Posthypnotic suggestion was used on both patients, prior to and during the operations. There was complete absence of pain during the postoperative period as well as in the course of the surgery. Both patients were discharged in good condition, one child after twenty days and the other in thirty days.

It is usually thought by uninformed laymen that only weak-willed or unintelligent people make good hypnotic subjects, but many researchers have found that those with strong minds and high intelligence make the best subjects. Such comments as these are made determinedly by most responsible practitioners, and yet about hypnosis no dogmatic statement should ever be made. I personally know a young New Jersey woman named Doris who is mentally retarded. When she was twenty-seven, with the mental age of about an eight year old, she had to have a large cyst removed from her buttock. It was an operation that could be performed in the doctor's office, if Doris would only cooperate. But she was not about to. She allowed no doctors, nurses, or other strangers close enough to her to touch her. It was impossible, therefore, for them to give her a local anesthetic.

Hypnosis worked on Doris. Beginning to speak to her very gently and soothingly, the doctor soon had her listening intently as he spoke of how sleepy she was becoming. It was not long until he had her somnambulized and receptive to the suggestion that she would let the nurse give her a hypodermic injection. She then went deeply asleep and felt no pain from the operation.

A good journalist should know his subject thoroughly, so Norman M. Lobsenz, when preparing an article for *Good Housekeeping* (June 1968), went the hypnosis route in order to be able to discuss it intelligibly. He wrote:

I recently got hypnotized to find out what it feels like. The "trance state" was not anything like what I expected. At all times I was completely aware of everything that was going on in the room, of street noises, and of my own thoughts. There was no sense of being "asleep," or "controlled." I was completely relaxed and had my eyes closed, but I felt as if I could get up and walk out any time I wanted to.

When I was given the usual suggestions—that I couldn't open

my eyes, or get up from my chair, or separate my entwined fingers—I thought, "This is ridiculous, of course I can!" But somehow it seemed simpler to "humor" the hypnotist.

For the same reason, Lobsenz says, he made his arm rigid and held it at right angles to his body for ten minutes without any strain. He was then told there was something written on an index card that he wanted to see, but that he wouldn't be able to hold the card because it was covered with oil. He knew that was silly, because he could see the card was clean; but as he tried to grasp it his fingers deliberately fumbled and dropped it—virtually pushed it away. Then he was told he would forget there was any number between six and eight, and though one part of him knew that seven existed, when he repeated the numbers from one to ten, he "decided" to leave seven out.

This is perhaps as good a description as one can get of the condition of a subject during light hypnosis. When hypnotized, you are not a zombie, unless you are in the deepest phases. You are perfectly aware of what is happening around you and can awaken yourself at any time. As Lobsenz has shown us, however, you just don't want to. You have a real desire to do what the hypnotist asks of you. You are conditioned by his expectations and attempt to respond as you think you should. Hypnotic states are classified as light, medium, and deep, but it has been discovered that there are also various stages in between. It is apparently safe for the vast majority of people—although, of course, not everyone should be hypnotized. If you are very disturbed or depressed, or have a history of psychiatric treatment, you should stay away from it unless it is recommended by your analyst.

When amateurs play with this as a game—and that is not

advised by anyone familiar with the subject—sometimes traumatic experiences may occur. Some students at a Midwestern university were age regressing one of their group purportedly to a past life, and they had exciting results when the sleeping girl began to speak a foreign language that no one present understood. She was age regressed on several occasions, and each time she went deeper and deeper into the role she was portraying. Finally she became the other entity so thoroughly that she lost awareness of her own identity and *was* the other person. (One theory is that she was actually possessed by the spirit of someone who spoke only the foreign tongue.) In that state she did not know English and did not recognize anyone present. Finally, at the last session, when the operator said, "You are slowly coming back to normal. When I count to ten you will open your eyes," she could not understand him. She continued to talk in this strange language, comprehending no English whatsoever. And she was unable to be awakened. The young people were quite alarmed, not knowing that the girl would most probably come to herself eventually by the normal process of sleeping it off.

This is not an isolated case. Amateur hypnotists fairly regularly run into situations with which they don't know how to cope. This is one of the reasons it is not wise to let a novice make such attempts with you.

Hypnosis is especially useful in psychoanalysis, doctors have found. In his book *New Concepts of Hypnosis*, Dr. Bernard C. Gindes says:

Hypnotism, stripped of its occult raiment [How can they expect the harlot to reform when they continue to treat her so disrespectfully?] is a method of therapy which seeks to dramatize thought into specific action for a definite end. Together with psychoanalysis, it is a means for acquiring information in areas that are not easily accessible by other methods. By this means we are in a position to release the negative effects of past traumatic experiences. When hypnosis is utilized for the animation of thought, we call this activation *suggestion*. It is the means by which a thought may be placed in the mind of a subject for directed or controlled reaction.

Gindes, surprisingly advanced in his thinking for a medical man, adds, "We have learned, too, that thoughts may control the functions of the human body." It has been discovered that they can cause changes in temperature, the regularity of the heart-beat, the rate of blood-pressure, and respiration. "Psychosomatics, a branch of medical science that recognizes a mental basis for physical ailments, makes the bold assertion," he says, "that eighty-five percent of illnesses, hitherto regarded as organic, are actually functional in origin; i.e., they result directly from the impact upon the body of a thought charged with emotion. This claim would seem fantastic were it not backed up by incontrovertible clinical data."

Repressed anger, painful experiences, forgotten fears all drop into the unconscious mind—which never forgets anything—setting up conflicts that result in functional disturbances of the system. Psychosomatic medicine, in order to discover the trauma which caused the disturbance, seeks to penetrate the unconscious mind through the study of dreams, word-associations, and hypnosis; and the last, says Gindes, "is by far the most direct route to the understanding and re-education of the unconscious."

We should consider some of the various ways in which hypnosis is induced. What is called "The Method of Explicit

Suggestion" or "Sleep-Suggestion Technique" is that used today by most practitioners in this country. It consists of telling the subject over and over in a progressive manner that he is relaxing, feeling drowsy, sleepy; that his eyes are heavy, tired, that they are closing, and that he is falling asleep.

Another technique developed in recent years is to have the subject visualize various scenes and concentrate on them. This is usually combined with suggestion and can be quite effective in some instances.

The "Fascination Method" proceeds from a single process, that of having the subject stare intently at an object so that intense ocular fatigue is created. Some hypnotists use their own eye as the object of fixation; others use a brilliant surface, such as that of a watch or a shining flashlight. The object is usually held directly above the subject's normal range of vision, so that he must strain his eyes slightly to bring it into focus. When ocular fatigue forces him to close his eyes, this provides the springboard for sleep suggestion.

Some people today still use the stroking and passes with the hands originally employed by early day mesmerists.

British psychiatrist Gordon Ambrose and London gynecologist and surgeon George Newbold, in *Hypnosis in Health and Sickness*, make great claims for hypnosis in the treatment of epilepsy, a variety of emotional disturbances, numerous disorders of women and children, dentistry, obesity, excessive smoking, homosexuality, and alcoholism. Their definition of the subject is especially helpful to our understanding. "Hypnosis," they say, "is an artificially induced state characterized by a heightened suggestibility. The hypnotized person appears to be conscious of his surroundings, but is in a state of 'fascination.' He is not asleep or unconscious; he understands and appreciates his surroundings, knows who he is and where he is; but is relaxed, deliciously sleepy, heavy in his limbs and altogether calm, comfortable and relaxed."

The most important thing to remember is that neither the hypnotist nor his subject are alone. The hypnotist has established a rapport, a sympathetic relationship, with his patient; indeed, he has joined his patient, in a sense, in facing and overcoming the problems the patient hitherto had faced alone.

So today the medical profession is pioneering in a new area of therapy that is proving most successful. Night club entertainers are providing fun and games with hypnosis as show biz people have for several centuries. And teachers of courses in autosuggestion are having a heyday. But what about those dark alleys and narrow streets of the past—the occult? It, too, has gone respectable. Today parapsychologists are using hypnosis as an experimental device for producing ESP. They have found that it makes the production of psychic phenomena, or psi, easier. Hypnotized persons quite often do significantly better in laboratory tests. As Dr. Thelma Moss said in *Psychic*, August 1970: "In a state of hypnosis, it seems the barriers go down. The subject usually loses his inhibitions about talking or saying whatever comes into his mind, which he might not do in a normal waking state." And thus his psychic talents may be revealed.

From the very beginning, hypnosis has produced fascinating manifestations for those who could bring themselves to look at them with unprejudiced eyes. As Lee Edwards Levinson pointed out in "Hypnosis: The Key to Unlocking Latent Psi Faculties": "The three most prominent somnambulists in history, beginning with Victor Race, the first clearly documented hypnotic subject, Andrew Jackson Davis, the 'Poughkeepsie Seer," and Edgar Cayce, all discovered their latent psi abilities after they had undergone hypnosis. Over the years, many experiments have been conducted by recognized investigators which offer ample proof that somnambulistic subjects under hypnosis display more acute extrasensory powers."

It is with these unusual powers and abilities, brought out more acutely through hypnosis, that this book deals. The most exciting and challenging areas of hypnotic research today are in parapsychology.

2. Lurid Past

HYPNOSIS IS nothing new. Throughout primitive and classical history we read where hands were passed over or laid on, where ailing citizens were successfully blown at or stared at or pointed at or commanded to be rid of a malady, or, conversely, where someone who had incurred the hatred of a witch doctor was programmed to come down with something. It is called magic in tribal societies, and shamans and magicians have used it ever since time began. Even in the Stone Age religious leaders or healers no doubt awed their cavemen audiences by going into self-hypnotic trances and producing various enchanting phenomena.

The all night dances of American Indians before a war party involved self-and-group hypnosis. Dancing to the monotonous beat of drums, the brave would be chanting in effect, "I am a great hunter," "I am a great warrior," and he would then go forward to face danger with heightened courage.

The Ebers Papyrus, more than three thousand years old, describes the use of hypnotic procedures by Egyptian soothsayers. In the temples of Isis, Nature Goddess of the Nile, Egyptologists have found numerous engravings showing worshipers in poses unmistakably characteristic of hypnotic trance. Priest-kings of the Two Lands used entranced virgins as message-bearers from the gods; and in biblical times the High Priests of Khem utilized mass hypnotism to still the mutterings of the people.

A Greek engraving ca. 928 B.C. shows Chiron, the most renowned physician of his time, placing his pupil Aesculapius under hypnosis. The Delphic Oracle and other contemporary oracles all operated in trance, either self induced or assisted by drugs or volcanic fumes.

Gindes says: "From every country, from every period of man's history, we find documents, paintings, sculptures and bas-reliefs attesting to the universality of the practice. In fact, there is adequate reason to believe that hypnosis in some form has appeared spontaneously and almost concurrently wherever human beings have congregated." Of course, ESP has too, but Dr. Gindes would not have been interested to comment on that.

Christianity made a clean sweep, and hypnosis and healing were gradually phased out of the churches. During the Dark Ages hypnosis fell completely into disuse in Western culture, except for certain bad guys like demon worshipers and heretics. During the latter part of the Middle Ages, however, outstanding men with highly imaginative minds began exploring every mental task available. Magic offered them as great an intellectual romp as any other unknown quantity, but at the same time they were investigating medicine, astrology, and alchemy. They considered the pursuit of the legendary philosophers' stone—that magical ingredient that would change base metals into gold—worthy of their best efforts; in their search for it, alchemists actually became the first chemists. They believed themselves to be on sound scientific grounds in their prospecting for gold, for within the framework of the then current knowledge its manufacture was a declared possibility. Everybody in those days went along with Aristotle's thinking, and this ancient Greek had stated that there existed a prime matter that was the basis of all substances in the terrestrial world. The interaction of matter and form, he believed, gave rise to the four elements: fire, air, water, and earth, which in turn, through their various combinations, produced all material objects. Thus, changes in the proportion of these elements resulted in changes in the form of the prime matter, and so, in theory, any substance could be transmuted into any other substance if the suitable conditions could be found. The only trick, then, was to find the right proportion of the right combination of elements, stir it correctly, add the proper dash of seasoning, and the ragout thus whipped up might make a man independently wealthy for life. However, alchemists had more up their long flowing sleeves than a mundane search for metals. They also wanted to discover "spiritual gold," or the proper unfoldment of the secrets of life—plus an elixir by which it might be prolonged indefinitely.

Tenuous as these quests were, they naturally attracted four-flushers, and the proliferation of those who claimed to know the secret of the philosophers' stone soon gave the entire profession of alchemy a bad name, which it has never entirely lived down to this day. Yet there were a few prominent alchemists who were so outstanding that they won the respect of their associates and a good report in history. One was born near Zurich in 1493 with the name Auroelus Philippus Theoprastus Paracelsus Bombast von Hohenheim. He chose to go down to fame under the abridged appellation Paracelsus, and perhaps it is just as well. He studied medicine, metallurgy, chemistry, and alchemy all over the eastern half of the world before settling down as a professor of medicine at the University of Basle. Paracelsus was killed while in his forties. Had he lived longer, he might have been able to materialize some of his unique concepts, which were considerably advanced for his age. Some of them were even advanced for ours.

It was this man's odd ideas about magnetism that brings him to our attention at this particular point. He is said to have employed a magnet in medicine, recommending its use, inasmuch as it attracted martial humors, in fluxes, inflammatory diseases, hysteria, and epilepsy. But for the most part, Paracelsus applied the term "magnetic," as a metaphor, to all action at a distance, real or presumed, between bodies of all kinds on earth. In medicine the principal mediator of this action he believed to be a somewhat eerie product called "mummy." As everyone surely knows, there are various kinds of mummy, but the most precious is the moss that grows on the skull of the criminal hanging on the gallows. In areas not sufficiently favored with criminals and gibbets, a scarcely less efficient mummy may be constructed at small expense from the blood, hair, nail clippings, and waste products generally of the human body. This, say alchemists, is the true Magnes Microcosmi and rightly used is competent for the cure of all diseases. Mummy so prepared from the living body might be given to an animal to eat, and the diseases of the original owner would then be transferred to the innocent dog or pig or rabbit. Or better still, mix the mummy of the sick person with earth and place in this earth seeds or plants, and as the plants grow they will suck up the mummial spirits, and the sick person will be cured.

If all this sounds a bit farfetched, remember that Paracelsus' writings were, to say the least, unsystematic, and his prescriptions were, no doubt by design, obscure. No use letting all the other alchemists in on your private secrets.

Toward the end of the sixteenth century, Paracelsus was worthily succeeded by another theoretician, J. B. van Helmont, a scientist of distinction in his day and an energetic proponent of magnetism.

"Material nature," he wrote, "draws her forms through constant magnetism from above, and implores for them the favor of heaven; and as heaven, in like manner, draws something invisible from below, there is established a free and mutual intercourse, and the whole is contained in an individual." Van Helmont believed also in the power of the will to direct the subtle fluid.

Robert Fludd, a well-known English magnetist, lived in the first part of the seventeenth century. He was an exponent of the microcosmic theory and a believer in the magnetic effluence from man. Not only, he thought, were these emanations able to cure bodily diseases, but they also affected the moral sentiments.

Another magnetist was the Scottish physician Maxwell, who is said to have anticipated much that Anton Mesmer later subscribed to as doctrine. He declared that those who are familiar with the operation of the universal spirit can, through its agency, cure all diseases, at any distance. He also very astutely suggested that the practice of magnetism, although very valuable in the hand of a well-disposed physician, is not without its dangers and is liable to many abuses.

While the theoretical branch of magnetism was thus receiving attention at the hands of philosophers and thinkers, the practical side was by no means neglected. There were in the seventeenth and eighteenth centuries a number of "divine healers" whose magic cures were without a doubt the result of hypnotic suggestion. Of these perhaps the most successful was Valentine Greatrakes, Esq. of Waterford, "in the kingdom of Ireland, famous for curing several diseases and distempers by the stroak of his hand only." This interesting man was born in 1628 and on reaching manhood served for some time in the Irish army, thereafter settling down on his estate to, as he presumed, retire. But in 1662 he had a dream in which it was revealed to him that he possessed the gift of curing king's evil. Now, in England, Scotland, and France, the idea that a touch of the royal hand was a sure remedy for scrofula had long been prevalent, and consequently this complaint had acquired the name of "king's evil." In France this practice dates from the reign of Louis IX and in England from that of Edward III, who is reported to have performed a considerable number of cures. He was wont to wash the affected part of the sufferer, but gradually the use of actual ablutions was discontinued—after all, kings have *some* dignity—and most subsequent rulers contented themselves with mere touching, while at the same time prayers were offered up on behalf of the patient.

Valentine Greatrakes' dream was repeated several times before he paid heed to it, but at length he made the experiment on his own wife—and healed her! Many who came to him from the surrounding country were cured when he laid his hands on them. Later the impression came on him strongly that he could cure other diseases besides king's evil. News of his wonderful powers spread far and wide, and patients came in hundreds to seek his aid. In 1666 he went to London, and although not invariably successful, he seems to have performed there a surprising number of cures, which were attested to by many eminent people. His method of healing was to stroke the affected part with his hand, thus driving the disease into the limbs and so finally out of the body. Even epidemic diseases he healed by a touch.

A simple and pious man, gentle and kind, and a stranger to all deceit, Greatrakes persuaded himself that his marvelous powers were a divinely bestowed gift, and he was most anxious always to make the best use of them.

Anton Mesmer, who is discussed in the next chapter, probably owed many features of his system to a Swabian priest named J. J. Gassner, who resided chiefly at Ratisbon in a southern duchy of Germany but traveled a great deal visiting many towns in Bavaria. His cures soon gained him wide repute as a great healer. All diseases, according to him, were caused by evil spirits possessing the patient, and his mode of healing was to exorcise the demons.

Gassner, too, was a man of kindly disposition and piety, who made large use of the Scriptures in his healings. The ceremony of exorcism was a rather impressive one, and some of his shocking techniques make interesting reading. Herr Gassner sat at a table with the patient and spectators in front of him. His fine personality, deep learning, and noble character inspired the faith of the patient and his friends, doubtless playing no small part in his healings. Sometimes he used magnetic manipulations, stroking or rubbing the affected part, and, in the manner of Valentine Greatrakes, driving the disease into the limbs of the patient and then out at the hands and feet.

The formula for exorcism he generally pronounced in

Latin, with which language the demons usually showed perfect familiarity. As an example of the fantastic techniques he used, once in Latin he commanded a young girl to go into trance. She responded instantly. Her left arm began to move slowly in answer to his "Agitetur bracium sinistrum." Soon it gained impetus, faster and faster, until Father Gassner boomed "Cesset!" The arm then dropped limply to the girl's side. Then it was suggested that she was going mad; her face contorted horribly, and she leaped about the room on all fours, displaying all the symptoms of mania.

"Pacet!" thundered the priest, and she stood quiescent. He then commanded her to speak in Latin, and she replied in Latin that she could not.

The climax to Gassner's treatment is difficult for us to accept, even though it is reported on good authority in several texts. He told the girl that her pulse was becoming very slow. The town's physician was there and felt her pulse and confirmed that it was truly beating slowly. Satisfied that the witnesses were impressed, Father Gassner suggested that the pulse leap and beat more quickly. Upon examination, it was then found to have risen fifty beats per minute beyond normal.

Everyone present was justifiably startled when the priest gave his next instruction. The girl was to lie quietly, then her pulse would beat slower and slower and finally cease. Her muscles would relax completely, and she would die for a short time. He told her that she need not fear; his powers would restore life to her body. And the gullible little fool did what she was told. She died. The physician took her pulse, with beads of perspiration on his forehead, no doubt, and pronounced her indeed deceased.

Confidently, Gassner then uttered the proper words to

bring her back to life and to consciousness. Her pulse began to beat again, her muscles jerked spasmodically, and then she sat up, rejoicing. She stated that she had been blessed by a miracle, reborn, that her pains had left her and that she was cured of all her ills. Whether this condition continued in the months and years to come is not reported. So with no further corroborating testimony, we do not recommend this technique for neophytes in the field. It seems a trifle extreme for beginners. Yet some yogis have been doing similar things to themselves for ages. Possibly Father Gassner had somehow latched onto their secret.

If the famous Mesmer did not actually meet Gassner— and there are statements to the effect that he probably did— he must nonetheless have been conversant with his methods of operation, particularly his more flamboyant ones. Mesmer was soon to burst upon the world as an exciting and entertaining phenomenon, and even, possibly a therapeutic one.

3. Mesmerism

Frank Podmore wrote in *From Mesmerism to Christian Science*:

The 11th of August should be observed as a day of humiliation by every learned society in the civilized world, for on that date in 1784 a Commission, consisting of the most distinguished representatives of Science in the most enlightened capital in Europe, pronounced the rejection of a pregnant scientific discovery—a discovery possibly rivaling in permanent significance all the contributions to the physical Sciences made by the two most famous members of the Commission—Lavoisier and Benjamin Franklin. Not that the report on Animal Magnetism presented by Bailly and his colleagues did serious injustice to Mesmer himself, or to his vaunted science. The magnetic fluid was a chimera, and Mesmer, it may be admitted, was perhaps three parts a charlatan. He had no pretensions to be a thinker: he stole his philosophy ready-made from a few belated alchemists; and his entire system of healing was based on a delusion. His extraordinary success was due to the lucky accident of the times.

Yes, the world had been ready for Mesmer. By then medicine, says Dr. Ginges

was failing miserably to meet the challenge of the new industrial age with its accompanying diseases. When medicine kills more patients than it cures, the hopeless multitude turns from the orthodox practitioner to the charlatan for relief.

A few doctors drifted away from the orthodox therapies in an energetic search for new cure-alls that would lure their wandering patients back, even inventing various far out gadgets they hoped would accomplish fantastic cures. At the dawning of the eighteenth century medicine was still more superstition than science; but patients were less credulous than they once were, and they would not accept the old time cures unless they really worked.

Medicine has always looked askance at any activity that suggests that the medical profession has much more to learn about the mysterious workings of natural powers within the body. Podmore says: "Instead of adopting a scientific attitude towards these obscure problems physicians took refuge beneath a cloak of pompous infallibility. Such an attitude has unfortunately throughout history made the medical profession ridiculous again and again, but it is in the field of mental and unorthodox healing with its accompanying phenomena that ignorance and prejudice reached a new peak among the doctors."

It was Franz Anton Mesmer who exposed this most strongly. This outstanding man was born on May 23, 1733 in the Swiss village of Weil, near Lake Constance. His father, a simple, religious man, was a forester. Mesmer's mother wanted him to enter the priesthood, and he was sent to a monastery for his education. At the age of fifteen he obtained a scholarship to the renowned Jesuit college at Dillingen in Bavaria. He took a degree with honors in 1765 and then went to the University of Vienna, where he was graduated in medicine in 1773. His Latin thesis on that occasion showed the influence of some of the great medical and alchemical names of the past, including Gassner and Paracelsus. Entitled "The Influence of the Stars and Planets as Curative Powers," it dealt with the possible influence of the planets on the human body and inquired whether the sun and moon and other heavenly bodies did not give out a subtle emanation or invisible fluid that affected all things including the human organism. He believed that this subtle substance could be derived from a magnet or lodestone and that all cellular structures had an affinity for the magnet. This is why he used the term "animal magnetism" for the system of treatment he later devised.

While professional contemporaries were still fumbling with their noxious draughts, and the saw and the knife, seeing only the gross physical body, Mesmer inquired into the mind and soul of man. The process he developed for healing was attributed to the action of a force emanating from the operator and radiating toward the patient. According to Mesmer, the look, the laying on of hands, the passes, even the breath can send to sleep (or awaken) the subject by causing muscular contractions or relaxation, exciting or paralyzing the vital functions and intellectual faculties, because they serve as vehicles for the force they transmit from one nervous system to another. He had great success using this technique on his patients, and soon the journals of the day were publishing stirring accounts of his successful healing of apparently hopeless cases.

In his beginnings he was a painfully conscientious, modest, and unambitious physician who treated his poor patients free of charge, disdaining honors or money. He soon changed. Perhaps his marriage to the aristocratic Frau Maria Anna von Posch, the widow of a high German official and Mesmer's senior by ten years, had something to do with his altered attitude. Because of her influential connections and her wealth, he was able to acquire elaborate equipment for his treatment rooms and to live royally. He had a spiritual passion for music and during this time established a Viennese salon, his first musical protegé being the twelve-year-old Mozart.

Then Mesmer left Vienna rather suddenly. It is hinted that there was trouble about one of his young lady patients, but nothing has been revealed about what kind of trouble—animal magnetism or animal passions. He traveled to various cities on the Continent for a few years, and then in 1778 he descended on Paris with his entire retinue. There he was very favorably received—by the public. Medical authorities reserved their opinion. His success was boundless, nonetheless, and he became the topic of every salon conversation. He used his animal magnetism, which soon acquired the name mesmerism, on thousands of invalids and helped a great many of them.

Soon all the rage, Mesmer was so busy he could not begin to treat everyone who came to him, and he had to devise some scheme whereby he could handle many people at once. For mass production he built in his lavishly furnished establishment a large circular vat, or *baquet*, as it was called, in which he could sit a number of patients at once. In the water in the vat a number of substances were mixed. Each patient held one end of an iron rod, the other end of which was in the *baquet*. And then the most extraordinary scenes began.

"Sardonic laughter, piteous moans and torrents of tears burst forth on all sides," according to a witness named Deleuze, Librarian of the Royal Botanical and Zoological Gardens. "The subjects were thrown back in spasmodic jerks, the respirations sounded like death rattles, and terrifying symptoms were exhibited. Suddenly, the actors of these strange performances would frantically or rapturously rush toward each other, either rejoicing and embracing, or thrusting away their neighbors with every appearance of horror."

In another room, which was padded, a different spectacle was presented. "There," says Deleuze, "women beat their heads against the padded walls or rolled on the cushion-covered floor in fits of suffocation." In the midst of this panting, quivering throng, Mesmer, dressed in a violet coat, moved about waving a wand. He would halt in front of the most agitatedly excited and gazing steadily into their eyes, while he held both their hands in his, bring their middle fingers into immediate contact to establish the communication. At another moment he would, by a motion of open hands and extended fingers, operate with the great current, crossing and uncrossing his arms with wonderful rapidity to make the final passes.

Violent as the treatment was, it became tremendously popular, and nobody was anybody until he had tried it. Numbered among Mesmer's acquaintances, and possibly among his patients, were Mozart and his family, King Louis XVI and his queen, and Empress Maria Theresa of Austria. Soon, according to Dr. Gindes "Mesmer's Haven became a showplace for those intoxicated with his sensationalism. Magnetism was no longer associated with curing the ills of the afflicted; it became an extravaganza, a three-ring circus. All that was lacking was the Barnum to exploit it! It is no wonder that to this day, Mesmerism is associated with quackery in the eyes of science!"

What helped along its bad reputation was the Commission. In 1784 the French government appointed an official committee to investigate Mesmer. It was composed of three renowned scientists: Benjamin Franklin, the celebrated astronomer Jean Sylvain Bailly, and Antoine Lavoisier, "the founder of modern chemistry."

These worthy gentlemen tested Mesmer's baquet, but so soberly and unemotionally that they weren't cured of anything. So they concluded that Mesmer was a fraud.

Public interest in animal magnetism was quickly quenched, and Mesmer returned to Lake Constance, where he devoted the rest of his life to the free treatment of the poor. He died in 1815. He never did think of himself as a fraud, and indeed, when one reads his words in his booklet *Mémoire sur la Découverte du Magnétisme,* certain significant sentences lead one to believe he was aware that he had discovered something of much greater significance than the mere curing of hysterical patients. "Sometimes," he says

the somnambulist may perceive the past and the future through an inner sense of his. . . . Man is in contact through this inner sense with the whole of nature and can always perceive the concatenation of cause and effect. . . . Past and future are only different relations of its separate parts. . . . We possess an inner sense that is in touch with the whole of the universe. . . . We possess the power of feeling the connection between events and beings in the universal harmony.

Little is said in the records about any possible supernormal feats of Mesmer's patients, even though his statements above reveal that he was aware they occurred. It was to subsequent mesmerists that all the highly controversial extrasensory manifestations became evident. A former student of Mesmer's, the Marquis de Puységur, gave identity to the phenomenon that came to be known as "artificial somnambulism," the deepest form of hypnosis, a state analogous to a peaceful sleep, in which unusual phenomena were frequently produced.

The same year as Mesmer's decline, the Marquis discovered a twenty-three-year-old uneducated peasant named Victor Race who possessed the strange ability of sometimes perceiving thoughts that de Puységur had been thinking but had not expressed, and even, at times, information that he himself did not know, revealing a sudden acquaintance with faraway milieus and events completely unknown to both of them. He outlined the treatment necessary for his own cure of inflammation of the lungs, and when it was administered he recovered promptly. "There is no need of my speaking to him; I simply think in his presence and he hears and answers me," the Marquis wrote.

The influential de Puységur, living in luxurious retirement on his estates near Soissons, amused himself by haphazardly mesmerizing peasants from the surrounding villages. Victor, who was a simple-minded youth in his natural state, hardly able to converse wih his superiors, was altogether different when in trance, speaking freely in appropriate language. When he was awake he could recollect nothing that had taken place when he had been in the trance.

"The line of demarcation," the Marquis wrote in his memoirs, "is so complete that these two states may almost be described as two different existences."

De Puységur discovered also that most of his somnambulic patients were able to diagnose the nature of their ailments and to prescribe the appropriate treatments, and some could also diagnose and prescribe for the ailments of others. He quotes an instance to show how this claim to diagnose maladies impressed spectators. Monsieur Cloquet, a collector of taxes in Soissons, had at de Puységur's request come over to see the magnetic treatments. After watching the somnambules going about and prescribing for the patients, he resolved to test the matter on his own account. De Puységur quotes his statement: "I got one of the 'doctors' (somnambules) to touch me," he said.

She was a woman of about fifty. I had certainly told no one the nature of my ailment. After paying particular attention to my head, the woman said that I often suffered pain there, and that I had constantly a buzzing in my ears—this was true. A young man who had been an incredulous spectator of my experiment then submitted himself for examination. He was told that he had obstructions in the abdomen, arising from an illness which he had had some years previously. All this, he told us, was correct. But, not content with this soothsayer, he went straight away to another "doctor," twenty feet distant, and was told exactly the same. I never saw anybody so dumbfounded with astonishment as this young man, who had assuredly come to ridicule rather than to be convinced.

This artificial somnambulism demonstrated by de Puységur was a definite step ahead of the hysterical outbursts occasioned in most cases by Mesmer. The Marquis was also the first to describe magnetism at a distance, which has in recent years come to be a mainstay of modern Russian telepathic research. Some of the peasants who visited him fell into a crisis as soon as they set out on the road when still a great way off. A manifest proof, he says, of the efficacy of the will in directing the fluid even at a considerable distance.

In October 1785, Captain Beatrix, an officer of artillery stationed at Metz, was directed by one of his patients to magnetize her at midnight when she was asleep in her own house. The husband, who carefully watched the while, inferred at the given time from the remarks made by his wife and her movements that she was in a veritable hypnotic state. Captain Beatrix was quite satisfied that the crisis was due to his own magnetism from a distance, and de Puységur was inclined to agree.

From this time on many researchers were using the techniques of mesmerism and achieving varying results, revealing already at this early date the fact that in this region the observer finds what he looks for. For years after mesmerism had been officially debunked, doctors experimented with it in various French hospitals. A young physician named Alexandre Bertrand began in 1819 to give a series of courses on animal magnetism, discussing the many curious aspects of it that were being discovered in Paris hospitals. During his researches he and his collaborators came upon a variety of aspects of hypnosis apparently for the first time in their experience. Magnetism at a distance was one. Scarring and injuring a patient without his feeling pain was another. A flask of ammonia was held to a subject's nostrils for fifteen minutes without any uncomfortable effect being produced. Clairvoyance of the patient's own diseased organs and prescribing for his own ailments appeared fairly commonplace in Bertrand's experience. Probably the first to break away from the magnetic theories of Mesmer, Bertrand described experiments in which he verbally commanded his entranced subject to do one thing while *willing* her to do the opposite. Unable to solve this conflict situation, the subject would show signs of increasing agitation, which Bertrand could not resolve except by making his willed and verbal commands coincide. He also found that willed instructions were sometimes as effective as verbal ones.

The Abbé Faria, a Portuguese monk who had learned hypnotic techniques during his travels in India, had for some years given public performances apparently much like the demonstrations of stage hypnotists today in night clubs and theaters, during which he made his subjects drink water thinking it was lemonade, see the phantoms of absent friends and talk to them, and so on. In 1819 he published a book, *De La Cause du Sommeil Lucide,* in which he maintained that the phenomena of the trance were to be attributed neither to a fluid nor to the will of the operator, but to self-suggestion on the part of the patient. Since Faria had no medical training, his ideas received little attention, even though they are nearer to the present-day concept than the beliefs of most others of his day.

Even so, the idea of suggestion caught on. Professor H. Bernheim and others of the Nancy School, a group of ardent researchers, became strongly convinced that induction did not depend on the use of what they considered to be the old-fashioned magnets of Mesmer. Bernheim declared that suggestion was the key to all such phenomena. There is no such thing as mesmerism, there is only suggestion, he maintained.

The famous neurologist Jean Martin Charcot, who lectured and taught at the Salpêtrière Hospital in Paris, became enthralled with the findings of other researchers and embarked on experiments of his own. He and his pupils succeeded in proving that there are several stages of hypnotic sleep and that the subject is capable of manifesting varying symptoms in each stage. Dr. Charcot, a man who was eminently sound in his own line, lent an air of authority to mesmerism. He had one mistaken idea that he clung to fiercely—that mesmerism was possible only with neurotic subjects. His experimentation had been limited to his own patients, who frequently had symptoms of morbid hysteria.

Not only did the Nancy School disagree with him about suggestion versus mesmerism, but they successfully demonstrated that mesmerism could be induced in normal subjects.

Despite Charcot's defeat to the Nancy School on many points, his influence on hypnosis was lasting, as much as anything because of all the brilliant pupils he influenced. One of his students at the hospital for a short time was Sigmund Freud, who was to use hypnosis with his first psychoanalytic patients but later was to discard it as too time consuming. Other pupils of Charcot and of the Nancy School who have been outstanding in hypnosis activity were Pierre Janet, Morton Prince, Baron Albert von Schrenck-Notzing, and Professor Charles Richet, all of whom were later to make significant contributions to psychical research, or parapsychology.

4. Channel Crossing

ALTHOUGH MESMER himself spent the years of the French Revolution in England, remaining there until about 1799, his presence seems to have made little impact, even on those interested in his system. In fact, it passed almost unnoticed. It was a French chemist and minerologist, Richard Chenevix, who finally made an impression with animal magnetism by bringing it to the attention of one of England's most prominent doctors. When Chenevix began practicing mesmerism in a military hospital, Dr. John Elliotson observed his techniques and became curious. Chenevix died after only a year in London, but in 1837 another Frenchman, Baron Du Potet, came to use his techniques on some patients at the University College Hospital. Inspired by what he saw, Elliotson took up the practice himself.

John Elliotson was a bold hero type. He occupied a considerable position in the medical world, being senior physician to University College Hospital, a professor of practical medicine at the University of London, and the president of the Royal Medical and Chirurgical Society. He was vigorous, unconventional, self-willed, and impetuous, even rather feisty it would seem, and his attitude toward his fellow doctors had never been conciliatory. He was the first to use the stethoscope in England, and he had forced on his profession many important additions to *materia medica*.

Elliotson was very popular with his students on personal grounds because he was a man of conspicuous ability and originality, an admirable lecturer and teacher—just such a man, one would say, to espouse the new cause of magnetism and cause it to flourish among the medical men in a new land. Instead, they murdered him! Figuratively speaking. He was made to suffer irretrievably for espousing such a detested cause.

The hostility of the medical profession was based on the fact that animal magnetism had a bad name, having in large part been practiced by imposters and quacks, or so it was believed. Many stories about the fantastic results with somnambulism in producing clairvoyance and other unbelievable phenomena were exaggerated, if not actually invented. Still, as it is stated in the Biographical Introduction in *Braid on Hypnotism*:

These were good ground for caution, but they were no grounds at all for passing over the evidence of those who were not charlatans, whose integrity and ability had never been questioned previously, whose statements were strongly documented. However, they were the rule of the moment, they justified a persecution which could not well have been more bitter if Elliotson had been a convicted cheat. They forced him to resign his professorship, they destroyed his practice, and there was a perceptible tone of triumph when his ruined prospects were recited.

In 1847 Elliotson reported the hitherto unknown phenomenon of "community of sensation," which he accidentally discovered to be a feature of the mesmeric rapport between himself and one of his patients. To the astonishment of several witnesses, he demonstrated the ability of a mesmerized subject to experience tastes, smells, and experimentally induced pains that he himself was experiencing, with no obvious contact between himself and the subject. As with his other experiences this report brought him denunciation. After he had resigned as chief physician of the University of London Hospital rather than give up the use of mesmerism as a medical tool, Elliotson began the publication of a journal called *The Zoist*, which appeared quarterly for over ten years. In it, recounting every story about successful hypnotism he came across, he carried on his battle with his medical colleagues, and later on with James Braid. The journal remains a source of great interest to scholars of hypnotism.

In 1865, when he was nearing eighty, Dr. Elliotson made a pathetic statement. He had found, he said, that neither he nor his disciples were any longer able to get results.

"I believe in what I originally saw," he stated to the chemist Benjamin Richardson, "mesmerism played the parts precisely that I claimed for it. It is a wicked error to suppose that I was a party to a deception, or to a whole series of deceptions, if you like; but I candidly say . . . that mesmerism, at the present moment, has no power to remove pain. It is a mystery; it had power, and I once saw a leg painlessly removed under its influence; but we are now in another cycle, and it seems to me that there are special periods only in which mesmeric phenomena can be induced."

Dr. Jule Eisenbud, professor of psychiatry at the University of Colorado Medical School, said in an article entitled

"Mesmerism, Hypnosis and Psychical Research":

Elliotson was quite correct in relating his latter day lack of success with hypnosis, as we now call it, to "cycles" of some sort. However, it wasn't hypnosis which had failed . . . but, in some way, Elliotson himself; and this failure was not due to purely external influence, as he supposed, but was more likely the result of subtle psychological and, in a strange fashion, parapsychological causes. It had happened to other people; it would happen again; it is happening still.

The next prominent doctor to espouse mesmerism was James Esdaile in India, in numerous brilliant demonstrations of painless surgery. An independently wealthy young medical man, Esdaile was, in 1845, in charge of a hospital for poor persons and criminals at Hooghly, near Calcutta. When he began to experiment on the natives under his charge, he found himself able to induce coma so profound that in some cases he could perform severe operations under its influence. Visitors who were allowed to witness some of these operations were impressed, so the government of Bengal appointed a committee to inquire into the matter. For it, Esdaile extirpated huge tumors, and his patients assured him they felt no pain during the operations. The report of the committee members was noncommital. They expressed the opinion that owing to the length of time required to produce a coma of sufficient intensity and the uncertainty of success, mesmerism would have little practical utility. When it is considered that Esdaile's technique required the patient to be treated for several days in succession and then worked on for perhaps four hours just prior to surgery and that even then a cough or any nervous idiosyncrasy of the patient might interfere with success, maybe the committee knew whereof it spoke.

The governor of Bengal, however, did not adopt the committee's skeptical attitude. He was more adventurous. Esdaile was appointed to a small hospital in Calcutta that would be under his exclusive control for a year. There he was able to make what experiments he wanted. At the end of his first year he was appointed Bengal Presidency Surgeon, one of the youngest men to hold the post, and he continued his practice for eighteen months longer in a hospital opened by public subscription.

During his six years' practice in India, Esdaile performed on mesmerized patients no fewer than 261 serious operations, such as cancers and amputations, and a large number of minor ones. Two hundred cases were for the removal of scrotal tumors varying in weight from 10 pounds to 103 pounds. Of these there were only sixteen deaths, although the mortality from the removal of similar tumors had previously been 40 or 50 percent.

The medical press in India, with its usual perspicacity, severely boycotted Esdaile and his operations and to the last persisted in regarding all his patients as deliberate imposters. When he returned to the British Isles he was no more successful. Still, his brilliant demonstrations of painless surgery undoubtedly would eventually have achieved recognition had it not been that ether and chloroform had just been discovered and were already used widely in surgery. Being considerably less trouble, taking much less time to administer, and producing sure results, these new drugs overpowered the evidence of the safety and freedom from unfavorable aftersymptoms when mesmerism was used.

Esdaile provided one of the earliest reports of the experimental induction of hypnosis by telepathy, claiming to have succeeded in mesmerizing a blind man on a number of occasions by gazing steadily at him from a distance of twenty yards. To safeguard against the possibility of giving sensory impressions, Esdaile used to stare at the man over a wall, often, as he stated, "at untimely hours, when he could not possibly know of my being in his neighborhood, and always with like results."

While Esdaile was doing his pioneering work in India, Dr. James Braid was beginning to be heard from back home. A warm-hearted, cheerful Scottish surgeon, Braid was practicing his profession in the English city of Manchester at the time. Having tried it on his own patients, he satisfied himself that there was something to all this mesmeric malarky. But he could accomplish it without magnets, by putting altogether different processes into action. Prolonged gazing on a brilliant object or any other equivalent maneuver was sufficient to produce in certain persons a numbness of the brain more or less deep, which rendered them capable of presenting the greater number of the phenomena until then attributed to magnetic influence. There was no reason, then, to postulate an unknown force. The operator did not send the subject to sleep; the subject sent himself to sleep as the result of the fatigue or exhaustion of his nerve centers. Later Braid discovered that eye fixation was not even necessary. He proposed a new name for this psychological condition, first calling it Neuro-Hypnotism and later altering it to hypnotism alone.

From 1842 on, Braid used this new technique in his own practice with beneficial results. Among the more striking cases he lists in his book *Neurypnology* are the cure or marked alleviation of long standing nervous headaches, neuralgia, tic doloreux, rheumatism, epilepsy, skin diseases, and many minor ailments, and the improvement of sight and hearing. The sobriety of Braid's views and his clear and convincing exposition gradually won some measure of recognition in the scientific community for hypnosis as a medical technique. It is curious to note that in contrast, Elliotson showed himself as hostile to Braid as to those of his critics who had rejected the mesmeric treatment altogether.

Braid died about eighteen years after he had first become interested in hypnosis, without any prescience of the verdict of posterity on his role in history—the "father of hypnotism" some called him. If he was that, who was Mesmer—the wicked fairy godfather?

Mesmerism now became more or less officially known as hypnotism, and it was understood that it could be produced by optical fixation and simple verbal suggestion. In this new garb, from which every trace of mesmeric showmanship had vanished, it started knocking all over again at the back door of science.

"For over twenty years," said Dr. Eisenbud

hypnotism remained on its good behavior while its advocates, still far from respectable in the eyes of the medical and scientific world, tried to explore its phenomenology within the limits of tolerable decorum. Then one of its investigators broke ranks. In 1876 William F Barrett, a Dublin Professor of Physics who later played a large part in the organization of psychical research in Britain, read a paper before the august British Association for the Advancement of Science (which had first refused it). In this paper the claim was again put forward that community of sensation between operator and subject, and remarkable clairvoyant phenomena (including "traveling clairvoyance"—in which a subject projects his mind to a distant scene and reports what is going on there) could indeed be observed with certain individuals under hypnosis.

The lid was off again, and for the next few years one report after another carried accounts of the baffling occult aspects of hypnotism. One of the first things the British Society for Psychical Research did, on its founding in 1882, was to appoint a committee to investigate mesmerism in general and its relation to thought-transference in particular.

It was good to have a professional society setting up rules for judging psychical phenomena. Many of the cases previously reported had been badly in need of more careful attestation. That fraud was frequently practiced we know on the testimony of Elliotson himself. In his valedictory address in the last issue of *The Zoist* he wrote: "Examples of clairvoyance abound, but though the phenomenon appears unquestionable we well know that gross imposition is hourly practiced in regard to it both by professional clairvoyants and private individuals influenced by vanity or wickedness. . . . The assertions of a clairvoyant should be believed . . . (only when) they are free from the possibility of lucky guesses or trickery, and are verified by ascertainment of the facts."

But when the facts seemed to point to a faculty of a more startling kind—the actual seeing of events at a distance—the evidence from that period is in most cases complete enough that we can feel fairly safe that it is accurate and that the situation was free of fraud. A good example of this kind of detailed report appeared in the *Bolton Chronicle*, September 8, 1849. Dr. J. W. Haddock set forth, with corroborative evidence, three cases in which a somnambulic patient of his, Emma, was instrumental in recovering lost property.

The cashier of a business firm in Bolton had to pay into the local bank a sum of 650 pounds. Some weeks later, on making up the accounts, it was found that the bank had no entry of the payment. Fruitless search was made at the bank, and finally as a last resource the cashier came with his principal to consult Emma, who, after correctly describing the missing papers—two bank notes and a bill—claimed to see them in an envelope with a number of other papers in a private room at the bank. Renewed search was made, and the missing notes and bill were discovered, having been inadvertently set aside among a number of unimportant papers.

On another occasion, G. Toulmin, the conductor of the *Bolton Chronicle*, consulted Haddock's clairvoyant as to the welfare of a friend named Willey who had gone to California. Full notes of the sittings were taken and printed immediately. Under hypnosis Emma gave a description of the doings and sufferings not only of Willey but also of his companion, Morgan. Among other details that could not have been derived from anyone present and that were verified later by correspondence, Emma saw Willey constantly rubbing his arms from rheumatism, and she expressed considerable alarm at seeing him climbing the rigging. He had, in fact, done so on one occasion to help furl the sails. She saw that Morgan had fallen overboard into the water and had a fever and that in the course of the fever he had had a vision of his wife. Willey himself, on his return to England, at a personal interview assured Haddock of the accuracy of all the facts. Unfortunately Haddock did not think it necessary to procure written attestation, but contented himself with merely recording the statements. It is still a good story because of the care Haddock took in making his reports.

Another account comes from Professor William Gregory, describing a visit paid by him to a friend in a town about thirty miles from Edinburgh. There he met a lady who had been twice mesmerized by his friend and who exhibited considerable clairvoyant powers. At Gregory's request, this lady

—she was personally unknown to him—began by giving him a minute description of his own house in Edinburgh. She then described his brother's house, near the same city, and his brother's occupation at the moment. Gregory continued with an account of the woman's traveling clairvoyance:

I now asked her to go to Greenock, forty or fifty miles away, and to visit my son, who resides there with a friend. She soon found him, and described him accurately, being much interested in a boy she saw playing in a field outside a small garden in which the cottage stood. It was some distance from town, on a rising ground. The boy was playing with a dog. I knew there was a dog, but had no idea of what kind, so I asked her. She said it was a large but young Newfoundland, black with one or two white spots. It was very fond of the boy and played with him.

"Oh," she cried suddenly, "it has jumped up and knocked off his cap." She saw in the garden a gentleman reading a book and looking on [everything she said about him was correct]. . . . Being asked to enter the cottage, she did so and described the sitting room. In the kitchen she saw a young maidservant preparing dinner, for which meal a leg of mutton was roasting at the fire, yet not quite ready. . . . On looking again for the boy, she saw him playing with the dog in front of the door, while the gentleman stood on the porch and looked on. Then she saw the boy run upstairs to the kitchen, which she observed with surprise was on the upper floor of the cottage, and receive something to eat from the servant, she thought a potato.

Professor Gregory wrote down every detail the woman said and sent the description to the gentleman to see if it could be corroborated. He learned that everything was exactly as she had described and had occurred as she had seen it, except that the boy had been given a biscuit by the cook instead of a potato!

5. Back Streets

To THOSE of us who have already familiarized ourselves with the literature of psychical research, there is no
stigma against the supernormal. In fact, it is the most interesting aspect of hypnosis to us. There is no use to deny it or
even to overlook it. It is in the records. It does occur, and it
presents challenges of interpretation and understanding. Yet,
face it, most who use hypnosis professionally today, and
practically all who write about it, ignore the historical data
relative to any manifestations that are unusual or phenomenal. They toss it off as lack of scientific objectivity in older
times, poor observation, or bad reporting.

It is true, of course, that such objections are valid in many
instances. Yet occasionally there is a well-attested historical
case that can hardly be overlooked without playing ostrich.
And much of the traveling clairvoyance, telepathy, and community of sensation that was reported from the early days of
mesmerism have since been duplicated. Today they sometimes even occur under controlled laboratory conditions.

So, to get our heads out of the sand, let us look at some of the better documented cases from France and England in previous centuries.

Podmore quotes a man named Townshend who was a better observer and recorder than most of his contemporaries and wrote a book called *Facts in Mesmerism* about some of his experiences. The highly critical Podmore did not quote Townshend's documentation of his cases, but seemed satisfied with it. Here is one of his accounts:

One evening, when sitting with my family, the idea occurred to me, "Could I mesmerize Anna M—— there as I then was, while she was in her own house?" to which I knew she was just then confined by slight indisposition. Acting on this thought, I begged all the party present to note the hour (it was exactly nine o'clock), and to bear me witness that then and there I attempted a mesmeric experiment.

This time I attempted to bring before my imagination very vividly the person of my sleepwalker, and even aided the concentration of my thoughts by the usual mesmeric gestures; I also at the end of an hour said, "I will now awake Anna," and used appropriate gestures. We now awaited with more curiosity than confidence the result of this process.

The following morning Anna made her appearance, just as we were at breakfast, exclaiming, "Oh, sir! did you magnetize me last night? About nine o'clock I fell asleep, and Mother and sisters say they could not wake me with all their shaking of me, and they were quite frightened; but after an hour I woke of myself; and I think from all this that my sleep must have been magnetic. It also did me a great deal of good, and I feel quite recovered from my cold after it. After a natural sleep I never feel so much refreshed. When I sleep for an hour in magnetism, it is as if I had rested a whole night." These were the words of Anna M——, noted down at the time as accurately as possible.

The English mesmerists also observed the community of sensation that had been commented on by French researchers. Innumerable illustrations of this are found in the literature of the period. There was later corroboration by rigorous experiments made by Mrs. Henry Sidgwick and Edmund Gurney of the Society for Psychical Research.

In Gurney's report in the *Proceedings* S.P.R., Vol. II, he says that the hypnotist was Mr. G. A. Smith and the subject was named Conway, who was in a "tolerably deep trance." Smith and Gurney stood behind Conway, without contact, preserving absolute silence. From time to time Gurney asked Conway whether he felt anything, but gave no hint or indication of whether he was right or wrong in his answers. A careful record was kept of everything said and done.

First Gurney pinched Smith's right upper arm. Conway at once showed pain, rubbing the exact spot on his own arm. Gurney pinched Smith's left arm. In a few seconds Conway rubbed the corresponding place on his own left arm, uttering strong complaints.

Smith put a succession of substances into his mouth. When Smith tasted mustard Conway said it was something bitter and rather warm. Cloves was described as some sort of fruit, mixed with spirits of wine, not like spice, tastes warm. Bitter aloes he said was not nice. Bitter and hot, harshness, not sweet, frightful stuff. Hurts your throat to swallow it. Bitter and salty. Sugar gave him a sweetish taste. Something approaching sugar. Powdered alum filled his mouth with water. Precious hot. Some stuff from a chemist's shop that they put in medicine. Something after the style of alum. When Smith was given cayenne pepper Conway showed strong signs of distress. "Oh! You call it good do you?" he cried. "Oh! give us something to rinse that down. Draws your mouth all manner of shapes. Bitter and acid, frightful. You've got some cayenne down my throat, I know." He entreated for water.

The subject was now awakened. He immediately said, "What's this I've got in my mouth. Something precious hot. Something much hotter than ginger. Pepper and ginger."

From Professor Fontan of Toulon we have an instance of transposition of special senses as told in his paper in *Revue Philosophique*, August 1887.

The subject, B., was a sailor, aged twenty-two, apparently robust, but suffering from hysteria with attacks of catalepsy. When he came under Fontan's care his left side was wholly devoid of feeling, the sense of smell was absent on that side, and sight and hearing were diminished. Hypnotic suggestion suspended the anesthesia for a few hours at a time, but the magnet, and the magnet only, removed it permanently, practically curing the patient.

During the time B. was under the doctor's care there were a number of transpositions of senses, the transposition of sight being, of course, the most bewildering of these supernormalities. It was suggested to the subject that he could see only with his fingers, and the psychical blindness he was undergoing was reinforced by placing a screen close to his face so that he could not see his own hands nor the objects offered nor the faces or gestures of any bystanders.

Printed letters were first tried, and the subject, who could scarcely read in his normal state, deciphered a few of these with difficulty. A number of skeins of colored wool, which he had never seen before, were then placed in front of him, and he was told to choose the red ones. He felt the wools, rejected unhesitatingly the colors not asked for, and arranged the red in a series. He also did this with the green and the blue wools when asked. The same experiments were repeated the next day with fresh specimens of wool. The room was completely darkened. B's. hand was placed in a box containing various patterns of wool, which he had never either seen or touched, and he was told to choose the blue ones.

"He seized them," says Fontan, "with such rapidity, such force, tossing aside all those which he did not want, that we supposed that the experiment had failed. Shut up in a dark room, where we could not see each other, we did not know what was going on, and fearing some access to frenzy, I precipitated myself on the subject and hypnotized him strongly, by pressing the globes of his eyes. He had had time enough during this scene, which did not last five seconds, to choose the wools and to hide them in his bosom. At no other time did he show such eagerness for the suggested color." He had, in fact, selected four blue skeins, which he clutched so closely that he had to be altogether inhibited before they could be taken from him.

Perhaps the best experiment of all was the next. The wools were placed on a table under a strong sheet of glass. B., psychically blinded and with the screen interposed, was told to place his hand on the glass and indicate the red wool. He resisted for a time, but "ended by consenting to search for the red wools, whose position he indicated by a tap on the glass, which left no room for doubt." He repeated this process several times with the green, the blue, and the yellow wools, and always with complete success.

Pierre Janet, an up-and-coming young psychiatrist and neurologist, had gone to Havre to investigate the claim of a leading physician there, Dr. Gibert, that he could entrance his pet subject, an elderly woman named Léonie B——, by merely willing her to sleep. Thoroughly skeptical at first, Janet soon found that he himself seemed able to accomplish a similar result on several occasions. One day he caught Gibert at a time when he was not in the habit of working with his subject. He asked the doctor to hypnotize Léonie then and there, Léonie at the time being in another house five hundred meters away. This attempt was completely successful, as Janet at once verified to his utter astonishment.

In a series of later experiments, which Janet reported some months afterward, Léonie was not only repeatedly hypnotized at a distance, and in the presence of six lay and medical witnesses, but was also made to carry out posthypnotic commands *mentally* given. Of twenty-one trials done over a period of days at distances of at least five hundred meters, no less than fifteen were adjudged complete successes. The times for the trials were picked by lot out of a bag by the observers. All trials in which Léonie was not found in deep trance when the investigators entered her house or in which the trance did not follow the mental suggestion within a quarter of an hour were counted as failures. The posthypnotic commands successfully carried out were simple acts such as going into another room and lighting a lamp in broad daylight.

Frederic W. H. Myers, who made a four-day stay at Havre in order to observe these experiments, wrote in *Human Personality and Its Survival of Bodily Death*: "Professor Janet was kind enough to allow me to peruse his notes, taken mainly at the actual moment of observation; and . . . I can vouch for the scrupulous care with which he has compiled his account of the case."

Myers described a series of experiments from April 20 to 24, 1886, observed by himself, his brother Dr. A. T. Myers, Dr. Gibert, Professor Paul Janet, Professor Pierre Janet, Dr. Jules Janet, Dr. Julian Ochorowicz, and M. Marillier. He wrote that these experiments were not easy to manage, since it was essential at once to prevent the subject from suspecting that the experiment was being tried and also to provide for her safety in the event of success. It was a responsible matter to bring this old lady in her dreamlike state through the streets of Havre, but that was what they hoped to do. It was necessary to provide her with an unnoticed escort, so several persons had to devote themselves for some hours to each experiment.

In some preliminary testing, on October 3, 1885, Gibert tried to put Léonie to sleep from the distance of half a mile. On checking, Janet found her awake. He hypnotized her to ask what had happened, and she said, "I know very well that Monsieur Gibert tried to put me to sleep, but when I felt him I looked for some water and put my hands in cold water. I don't want people to put me to sleep in that way; it makes me look silly." On October 9 Gibert succeeded in a similar attempt. She said in trance, "Why does Monsieur Gibert put me to sleep from his house? I had not time to put my hands in my basin."

Myers wrote about the April 1886 experiments as follows:

On the morning of the 22nd . . . we . . . selected by lot an hour (11 A.M.) at which M. Gibert should will, from his dispensary, which is close to his house, that Madame B. (Léonie) should go to sleep in the Pavillon. It was agreed that a rather longer time should be allowed for the process to take effect, as it had been observed that she sometimes struggled against the influence, and averted the effect for a time by putting her hands in cold water, etc. At 11:25 we entered the Pavillon quietly, and almost at once she descended from her room to the salon, profoundly asleep.

They all dined with Gilbert that evening, and another attempt was made to put the woman to sleep at her home and to bring her to his home by an effort of will. At 8:55, Gibert retired to his study, and Ochorowicz, Marillier, Janet, and A. T. Myers went to the Pavillon and waited outside in the street, out of sight of the house. At 9:22 they observed Madame B—— coming halfway out of the garden gate and then retreating. She was plainly in a somnambulic state and was wandering about and muttering. At 9:25 she came out (with eyes persistently closed, so far as could be seen), walked quickly past the group of doctors without noticing them, and made for Gibert's house, although not by the usual or shortest route. She avoided lamp posts, vehicles, and so on, but crossed and recrossed the street repeatedly. After eight or ten minutes she grew much more uncertain in her gait and paused as though she would fall. Myers noted the moment. It was 9:35. At about 9:40 she grew bolder and at 9:55 reached the street in front of Gibert's house. There she met him, but did not notice him, and walked into his house, where she rushed from room to room. Gibert had to take her hand before she recognized him. Then she grew calm.

Gibert said that from 8:55 to 9:20 he thought intently about her, from 9:20 to 9:35 he thought more feebly. At 9:35 he gave up the experiment and began to play billiards, but in a few minutes he began to concentrate on her again. It appeared that his visit to the billiard room had coincided with her hesitation and stumbling in the street.

Léonie was subsequently studied by Dr. Charles Richet, professor of physiology of the Faculty of Medicine of the University of Paris, who successfully duplicated the results of Janet and Gibert. Once when she was in Le Havre, the doctors sent her on a "psychic excursion" to Paris to see Richet. After a few moments she began to cry out in great agitation, "It's burning! It's burning!" She was referring to Richet's laboratory, which, it was subsequently ascertained, was, in fact, damaged by fire at that time.

Dr. E. Gley of Paris contributed to *Tribune Médicale*, May 1875, an account of experiments made by his friend Dr. Dusart. The subject was a hysterical girl of fourteen who Dusart found very susceptible to hypnotism. He early noticed that his passes were ineffective if his attention was not strongly directed to the desired result, and this gave him the idea to try the effect of purely mental suggestion. One day, before the usual hour for waking the patient had arrived, he gave her the mental command to awake. The effect was instantaneous; the patient woke and began her hysterical screaming. The doctor took a seat with his back to her and conversed with others, without appearing to pay any attention to her; but when he silently gave her the mental suggestion to fall again into the trance, his will was again obeyed.

After this, he made more than one hundred experiments of this sort under various conditions, and with uniform success. On one occasion Dusart left without giving his usual order to the patient to sleep until a particular hour next morning. Remembering the omission, he gave the order mentally, when at a distance of seven hundred meters from the house. On arriving next morning at 7:30 he found the patient asleep and asked her the reason. She replied that she was obeying his order. He said, "You're wrong; I left without giving you any order." "True," she said, "but five minutes afterwards I clearly heard you tell me to sleep until eight o'clock."

After a time Dusart discontinued his visits, and the girl's father hypnotized her instead. Nearly a fortnight after this change, it occurred to the doctor when at a distance of ten kilometers to try whether he still retained his power, and he willed that the patient should not allow herself to be entranced. Then after half an hour, thinking the effect might be bad for her, he removed the prohibition. Early the next morning he was surprised to receive a letter from the father —who would not be surprised to get a letter so promptly!— stating that on the previous day he had only succeeded in hypnotizing his daughter after a prolonged and painful struggle, and that, when finally entranced, she had declared that her resistance had been due to Dusart's command and that she had only succumbed when he permitted her.

Another report, from a very active investigator—Dr. Dufay—comes from *Proceedings* S.P.R., Vol. VI. Madame C—— of Blois was thirty-five years of age, of a nervous temperament, and slightly rheumatic. For some time she had been subject to periodic attacks of headache and sickness, and when usual remedies failed to relieve her, Dufay did not hesitate to try magnetism.

He began to discover that hardly had he pulled the doorbell when Madame C—— fell into a calm sleep. It was quite a different thing if anyone else rang the bell, for then she complained of the noise that was splitting her head.

Later she felt his approach from the further end of the street: "Ah! what happiness!" she would say. "Here is the doctor coming. I feel myself cured!" Sometimes her husband would try to encourage her by telling her he saw the doctor coming when it was not true, but she always knew, and the sickness continued until he really was coming.

"In a case of this sort, how could I hesitate to make an attempt at influencing her from a distance?" asks Dufay. "Moreover, I was driven to it by circumstances." At the height of one of her attacks, her husband came for him, but he was with a patient he could not possibly leave. So he assured Monsieur C——, without being in the least certain of it himself, that his wife would be asleep and cured when he got home again. And she was.

Later one night when Madame C—— was in perfect health, her name happened to be mentioned in the doctor's hearing, and the idea struck him that he would mentally order her to sleep. An hour later he went to her house and asked the servant who opened the door whether an instrument he had mislaid had been found there.

"Is not that the doctor's voice I hear?" asked Monsieur C—— from the top of the staircase. "Beg him to come up. Just imagine," he said, "I was going to send for you. Nearly an hour ago my wife lost consciousness, and her mother and I have not been able to rouse her."

Dufay did not dare to confess himself guilty of this catastrophe, but he was betrayed by the patient. "You did well to put me to sleep, Doctor," she said, "because I was going to allow myself to be taken away on a drive to the country, and then I shouldn't have been able to finish my embroidery."

Dufay also succeeded in putting Madame C—— into mesmeric trance during his vacation when her husband wired him for help when she had an attack.

One more French telepathic study follows—this from Professor Béaunis, a physiologist who had been working with the Nancy School.

"The subject," wrote Béaunis, "is a young man, a very good somnambulist, healthy, a little timid." He arrived at the home of Dr. Liébeault with his cousin, a girl who was also a very good somnambulist, who was being treated by hypnosis for a nervous condition.

Liébeault entranced the subject and said to him during his sleep: "At your awakening you will carry out the act that will be ordered *mentally* by those present." Béaunis then penciled these words on a piece of paper and showed them to Liébeault and some others present. It read: "Kiss his cousin." Everyone was careful not to say or do anything that would give this away, but they concentrated on it mentally as the boy came out of trance. After a little while he laughed and hid his face in his hands.

"What's the matter?" asked Béaunis.

"Nothing."

"What are you thinking?" No response.

"If you don't want to say it out loud, whisper it in my ear."

"Kiss my cousin," he whispered.

The report states that once the first step was taken, the rest of the mental suggestion was carried out with good grace.

6. Dark Alleys

MORE THAN FIFTY YEARS ago, psychologist William McDougall, later to become, with Dr. J. B. Rhine, founder of the Parapsychology Laboratory at Duke University, pointed out that the interest in spiritualism, "with all its abuses, and the charlatanism that accompanies such nebulous ideas and movements" involved hypnosis "in a mass of fraud and superstition, and, for the popular mind, drove it back to the region of the marvelous, the supernatural and the dangerous, made it, in fact, once more a branch of the black arts."

It is a strange (and perhaps significant) thing that when you start playing around with trances—whether hypnotic, mediumistic, or self-imposed—you invariably begin to receive data that claim to come from alleged spirits of the dead. This is what occurred with mesmerism, and it has been going on ever since wherever much trance work has been done.

Podmore wrote:

When table-turning and spirit-rapping were introduced into England from America, the mesmerists soon identified the mysterious force which caused the phenomena with the mesmeric or neuro-vital fluid. A little later, when the trance and its manifestations were exploited in the interests of the new gospel of Spiritualism, many of the English mesmerists, who had been prepared by the utterances of their own clairvoyants for some such development, proclaimed themselves adherents of the new faith.

Before his death Dr. John Elliotson became a convert to Spiritualism. J. W. Haddock, whose work on somnolism reached its second edition in 1851, did much to reawaken interest and divert attention from mesmerism proper to Spiritualism.

"The mesmerists generally," says Podmore, "found the marvels of the magnetic fluid insignificant in the face of the new revelation. Mesmeric operators became spiritual healers, and their subjects trance mediums; the Spiritualist platforms were thronged with magnetic clairvoyants who had developed into 'inspirational' speakers. The two movements naturally became identified in the minds of the public, and shared in a common condemnation. No physician who valued his professional reputation could afford to meddle with the subject, and the study of the induced trance and its attendant phenomena was relegated to oblivion," in England, at least, for more than a generation.

Yet as early as 1788 members of a research society in Stockholm had corresponded with the society at Strasbourg founded by de Puységur for the study of magnetism . . . and —about this same topic—communication with the dead. They stated that they had for some time been receiving through the mouths of their somnambules news of the spirit world and of their friends and acquaintances recently deceased. For the assurance of the friends at Strasbourg they sent extracts from their journals recording the conversations held. In the presence of the Prince Royal, several members of the nobility, and other distinguished persons, questions were put to two or three somnambules. The intelligences answering through the mouths of the entranced women professed in each case to be spirits who undertook in several cases to prescribe for diseases, even of persons not actually present in the room.

Similar occurrences were also prevalent at the time in other areas of Scandinavia and in Germany. The German physician Justinus Kerner discovered in somnambule Frederika Hauffe a subject who produced such significant material that he eventually wrote a book about her called *The Seeress of Prevorst.* Frau Hauffe could apparently see and converse with the spirits of the dead and also gave evidence of prophetic vision and clairvoyance. Many physical phenomena were witnessed in her presence: movement of objects without the contact of any human being, knockings, rattling of chains, and general poltergeist activity.

The seeress of Prevorst was apparently able when magnetized to see ghosts and to experience astral travel, now known as out-of-body experiences, and some of her activities brought a certain amount of evidence that her consciousness had been where she was aware of being, while her body was back home on her bed. Today we consider traveling clairvoyance, of which we have already spoken, to be a form of out-of-body travel, and she gave evidence of it on numerous occasions.

The name "Frau Hauffe" would cause one to expect a typical middle-aged, large-hipped German *hausfrau* with an apron She was actually a petite girl in her twenties when her strange psychic adventures were reported. Instead of looking characteristically German, she had Oriental features.

Justinus Kerner was a very well-known German poet and author, as well as a physician, when he came under the spell of this young woman of myriad psychic talents who so captured his curiosity and interest. He had his clinic (hospital) in the town of Weinberg, which was near Frederika's home. That is why she was taken to him when her "spells" became severe. Kerner was a pragmatist who did not believe in such things as trances and spells, and he had heard of her reputation; therefore, he was very reluctant to accept her as a patient. When he did, he refused for a long while to pay any attention to the suggestions for the correct treatment of her condition that were made through her, allegedly by a spirit doctor, when she was in hypnotic trance. Eventually she became so ill, however, that Kerner was forced to try to cure her in her own way. She was what he termed "highly magnetic," meaning that she was always in a hypersensitive state. We can recognize now that she was one of the great natural clairvoyants of all times, but Kerner did not realize this until long after he began to work with her.

The daughter of a forester, Frederika grew up more like a wood sprite than a typical child. Perhaps it was for this reason that the idea of marriage appalled her. The man to whom she was betrothed was not too old for her nor was he unhandsome; but she cried for six weeks after the engagement was announced and did not eat or sleep. This would hardly be invigorating for even a most sturdy citizen, and to Frederika it was the beginning of her end. Even though she lived several years longer, she was never to recover her youthful vitality.

Apparently the relationship between Frederika and her

husband was always good, but she was unable to be happy in the married state. Then her first child died soon after birth, and from that time she went downhill physically. Physicians and friends advised her to have another baby right away— but even in those days it took nine months. Her second child lived, although having it did not help her condition.

It was then that Kerner entered the picture. Although there was not a great deal he could do to help this unusual patient, when he finally became convinced of the genuineness of the phenomena she exhibited, he kept a day by day record of her every act and statement as well as her physical state. When he eventually began to treat her according to the trance directions—laying on of hands and very small doses of certain particular medicines—her condition improved. He said later he was ashamed to realize that the unseen physician was so much wiser than he.

Frederika could see ghosts, and for the sake of evidence it is good to learn that those around her could also see them on occasion. Even Kerner once saw one of them. To him it looked like a pillar of vapor about the size of a man. She described it in more detail as a tall old man.

About nine o'clock on the evening of May 2 (the year was probably 1826 or 1827), Frederika, contrary to all usual procedure, fell into magnetic sleep, although she had already experienced it once that day. But it was an unusual day because her father was extremely ill, and she was quite disturbed about it. She apparently went out of her body and was heard to cry, "Oh, God!" It sounded more like a breath than an overt exclamation. She awoke as if this outcry had startled her and said that she had heard herself double, as if two of her had spoken. At ten o'clock, still in the somnambulistic state and just before she fell into natural sleep, she said,

"God, lead Thou him now by your hand. He is sleeping softly in your arms."

The next morning the news was brought that her father had died at Oberstenfeld at eight the night before. About an hour after he died, at approximately the same time that Frederika had left her body, Dr. Fohr von Bottwar, her father's physician, was still in attendance and was then in a room next to the one where the body lay. With him was the dead man's brother, who heard nothing unusual. But while the doctor was sitting there he heard, "Oh, God!" distinctly pronounced several times from the death room; so he went in to investigate. He found only the stark and still body. Frederika's uncle had not heard the voice.

Dr. von Bottwar wrote to Dr. Kerner as follows:

After my arrival at Oberstenfeld I found Mr. Wanner already dead. However, when I was in the living room next to the room where the body lay, at nine o'clock at night, I clearly heard a voice in there call out, "Oh God!" I thought it was the dead man speaking. After I heard it for the third time I went into that room, thinking that possibly Wanner had not really been dead and that I had made a mistake, for I could not believe anything else but that this call had come from him. I therefore examined the body very painstakingly and remained for another hour to make absolutely sure that he was indeed dead.

Frau Hauffe expressed herself on this same experience:

Because of grief and thinking about my father's illness, because of the premonition of his death and the desire to know instantly how he was, I was so overtaxed that I was at once put into a condition where my soul . . . could go out of my body. . . . That whole day I had exerted all my influence on that distant doctor, praying God to inspire him to find a means to save my father. This I did especially just before my soul stepped out of my body. This is probably the reason that he alone heard my cry.

In France the most remarkable case of purported spirit communication through a magnetized subject occurred some years later, on the eve of the outbreak in America of the Spiritualist movement. Alphonse Cahagnet was a cabinet maker and restorer of old furniture who lived on the Rue St. Denis. He practiced mesmerism first for curative purposes. But one of his early somnambules, Bruno, fell into deep trances or ecstasies in which he professed to see the spirits of his deceased friends and on occasion to be admitted into heaven. Cahagnet appears to have had some acquaintance with the works of Emanuel Swedenborg, the great Swedish mystic and spiritual traveler to other realms, and Bruno gave accounts of his visions of heaven much similar to Swedenborg's. His revelations never went into areas where evidence could be procured, and the experiments with him ceased after a time.

Cahagnet soon found other subjects, all of whom experienced similar ecstatic visions and gave like descriptions of celestial scenery. The most remarkable was a young woman named Adèle Maginot, who had been a natural somnambulist from her childhood. She came to Cahagnet in the first place so that he might cure her of the problem of these spontaneous attacks because they were impairing her health. He soon found that she had remarkable gifts for diagnosing and prescribing for disease in others, and he employed her for a time in that capacity.

It soon appeared that Adèle could see not only her own deceased relatives but the friends and relations of other persons who came to consult her. As proof that the invisible persons with whom she allegedly communicated were who they said they were she would give descriptions of the dress of the deceased and the manner of his death. Cahagnet kept careful notes of what she said and afterward drew up an account of the interview, which he submitted to the inquirer or sitter for his attestation. These reveal that the descriptions were in some cases so detailed and exact and successful that they were phenomenal. An example:

M. Petiet asked for M. Jerome Petiet. Adèle described a young man whom she said she saw: about twenty-six years of age; not as tall as his brother; auburn hair; rather long, open forehead; arched and very pronounced eyebrows; skin very white and delicate; medium sized round and dimpled chin. She spoke of his clothing and then of his disposition: he was stubborn, selfish, without any fine feelings, had a sinister look, was not very communicative, and had but little affection for anyone. Everything said about him was acknowledged as true. It is to be wondered that his brother would care to contact such an unpleasant character, but for the sake of evidence it is good that he did. Even then the brother's vengeful nature prevailed. He made Adèle so aware of his physical pains at death that Cahagnet had to release her by passes because of her terrible suffering.

Still, just in case she had acquired her information telepathically from the mind of the sitter—a suggestion frequently still proposed to explain alleged spirit communication—tests were devised by other sitters that would exclude thought transference. Pastor J. J. Rostan wanted to obtain some evidence from Adèle that could not possibly be attributed to his own knowledge, so before he left home he asked his maid to give him the name of one of her acquaintances who had been dead for some time. He arrived at the séance armed with the name of one Jeanette Jex. Adèle in trance replied: "I see a woman who is not tall. She may be between thirty and forty years of age; if she's not hump-backed she must be crook-backed, for she carries herself very badly. Her hair is auburn; she has small gray eyes, a thick nose. She is not good looking, with a prominent chin, receding mouth, thin lips. Her dress is countrified."

Her costume was described and also the symptoms of her last illness. When Rostan handed the report to his servant later and returned it to Cahagnet after adding his signature to the account, he appended the remark: "This is correct as regards stature, age, dress, carriage, the disease and deformed figure."

7. American Advent

THE MARQUIS DE LAFAYETTE was very enthusiastic about mesmerism, and he shared his interest in it with the American colonists. They had already heard of animal magnetism for some years before it began to be practiced among them. They read the London newspapers regularly and often saw there long accounts of the miraculous cures Mesmer was effecting in Paris. The colonial newspapers of New York, Boston, and Philadelphia also carried reports on Mesmer's work, particularly when the French committee on which Benjamin Franklin served labeled Mesmer a fraud.

The first tangible introduction of the subject into the United States seems to date from 1815, according to Dr. Joseph Du Common, who delivered three lectures on magnetism in the Hall of Science, New York City, on July 26 and August 2 and 9, 1829. Du Common, a Frenchman, was then in this country as a teacher of French at the United States Military Academy at West Point. At those well-attended lectures he hailed animal magnetism as "a subject of vital importance to human happiness and life, and one which has given rise in Europe to vivid controversies." Through this man's efforts a society of magnetizers was formed, which soon grew to twelve members, including two doctors of medicine, all of whom practiced magnetism on patients who consulted them. Apparently some remarkable cures were achieved.

According to a most comprehensive coverage of the early American hypnosis scene by Allan Angoff in "Hypnotism in the United States 1800–1900":

A great American physician, Dr. Charles Caldwell (1772–1853) of Louisville, Kentucky, a colleague of the even more famous Dr. Benjamin Rush, returned from Europe an enthusiastic champion of the new science. Caldwell had observed mesmerizers at work in Europe, and he was deeply impressed, for he wrote in his book *Facts in Mesmerism and Thoughts on its Causes and Uses,* . . . "Never has there been before a discovery so easily and clearly demonstrable as mesmerism is, so unreasonably and stubbornly doubted, and so contumaciously discredited and opposed. . . . Yet never before has there been made, in anthropology, a discovery at once so interesting and sublime—so calculated to exhibit the power and dominion of the human will—its boundless sway over space and spirit. . . ."

Mesmerism was also encouraged in the United States when Thomas C. Hartshorn of Providence, Rhode Island translated a book by J. P. F. Deleuze of France entitled *Instruction pratique sur le Magnétisme Animal.* In his appendix to the translation, Hartshorn gave information about some cases of mesmerism as practiced in Providence at that time, for example, an interesting one concerning a nine-year-old girl named Anne who was attending the school of a Miss

Snow. During recess, when the child was found asleep, Miss Snow and others tried unsuccessfully to rouse her. They became alarmed and called in a young medical student, who saw at once that the sleeping child was in a magnetized state. Another little girl, Jane Bell, then burst into tears and confessed that she had put Anne to sleep and that she had done it several times before.

Hartshorn told also of the case of a physician, Dr. Brownell, who had a somnambulistic patient who could diagnose the illnesses of others. He asked her to examine a patient who had been ill for a long time with an unknown complaint. The somnambulist replied: "He looks so bad, I do not like to do it." The doctor asked her to look at the man's stomach, and she replied that it looked all right to her, as did his kidneys and liver and intestinal canal. But then she said that his spleen was very much enlarged. When Brownell asked how she knew, she replied: "It's a great deal larger than yours."

This woman had never studied anatomy nor seen pictures of the abdominal organs, and the patient himself was a mile and a quarter away; but seven days later he became seriously ill and died. Before the post mortem Dr. Brownell told all the sixteen physicians there the details he had received from the somnambulist—a very brave thing to do. The doctor then opened the abdomen, and, to the amazement of all present, found a spleen so enlarged it weighed fifty-seven ounces rather than a normal four to six ounces. No other disease was discovered in the man.

Providence and Pawtucket were apparently hospitable centers for experimenters in animal magnetism during the early nineteenth century, for so many cases come from that area. Thomas H. Webb, the editor of the Providence *Journal*, the leading newspaper, was keenly interested in the subject and reported much about it. Here is a case from his paper:

A Miss Jane C. Rider, apparently of Providence and known as both a clairvoyant and somnambulist, was the patient of the prominent Professor L. W. Belden, who stated:

On November 10, it was proposed to ascertain whether she could read with her eyes closed. She was seated in a corner of the room, the lights were placed at a distance from her, and so screened as to leave her in almost entire darkness. She read with great ease a great number of cards, some of which were written with a pencil and so obscurely that in a faint light no trace could be discovered by common eyes. . . . She told the date of coins, even when the figures were nearly obliterated. A visitor handed her a letter, with the request that she would read the motto on the seal, which she readily did, although several persons present had been unable to decipher it without the aid of a lamp. The whole of this time, the eyes were, to all appearances, perfectly closed.

Sometimes, the report goes on, a second handkerchief was placed below the one that she constantly wore over her eyes when being tested. (Funny the doctor did not think to mention that in the paragraph quoted above.) Once a Negress came in and seated herself beside Miss Rider, who was asked if she knew the lady. She smiled and returned no answer. Someone said: "She has a beautiful complexion, has she not?" Miss Rider laughed heartily and said: "I should think she was somewhat tanned."

A Miss Loraine Brackett of Rhode Island, when in trance, "could accompany any individual with whom her magnetizer placed her in communication to scenes that she had never beheld, hundreds of miles from the bounds of her furthest travels. She would then describe correctly what she saw in places where she had never been."

A woman of Milford, Massachusetts, in 1842 suffered

from a form of spinal disease that confined her to her bed. Her physicians regarded her ailment as incurable, but mesmerism healed her completely in six weeks and made it possible for her to walk several miles with ease.

About this time came Andrew Jackson Davis, a phenomenon of the times. Born in Blooming Grove, Orange County, New York, a child of impoverished parents, he grew up with very little education. His father was an uneducated shoemaker, and the family traveled so much that the boy attended school for less than five months in his life. In 1843, when Davis was seventeen years old, Professor J. Stanley Grimes, a well-known lecturer on mesmerism, gave a performance in Poughkeepsie. The youth, who lived there at that time, volunteered, but when Grimes tried to hypnotize him he was unsuccessful.

After the professor had left, however, a tailor, William Levingston, made a similar attempt on young Davis and sent him into trance. It became almost immediately obvious that he had the power of clairvoyance, for he could read a newspaper that was placed to his forehead, out of range of his vision, and he diagnosed disease. So they went into the clairvoyance business. For about eighteen months this team remained together, prescribing for all who came for consultation. In the somnambulistic state Davis claimed that the human body of the patient became transparent to his spiritual vision. He could see the blood and nerves. He could also trace every fiber in leaves and trees and see the veins of metal as rivers of fire running under the earth. He began to be referred to, not surprisingly, as "the Poughkeepsie Seer."

Andrew Jackson Davis also began to make philosophical statements so wise that they could not possibly have come from his conscious mind and hardly from his unconscious.

Listeners became fascinated and began to write down what he said. The aim of the messages was so exalted, the style and thought so impressive and dignified that many prominent and intelligent people were quite impressed. Since his "clairvoyant clinic" was only modestly successful, Davis soon abandoned the art of healing and turned to writing. He lectured and wrote while in trance, and it is said that during a two-year period in New York City he delivered 157 lectures in trance. All were copied verbatim by a scribe he had engaged for the purpose, the Reverend William Fishbough. All this resulted in his publication in 1847 of *The Principles of Nature, Her Divine Revelation and a Voice to Mankind.* This went into thirty-four editions in less than thirty years. Another book, *The Great Harmonia,* ran to forty editions. During his long life—he lived to be eighty-four—he wrote more than thirty full-length works.

His mission, revealed to him when in hypnotic trance by, he believed, Galen and Swedenborg, was the prophesying of a new dispensation preceded by a social revolution. In 1850 Davis and his followers identified themselves with Spiritualism. Trying to free it from the bad reputation it had been invested with by unscrupulous and capricious exploiters, he wrote: "Spiritualism, of the materialistic type . . . seeks the most evanescent evidences. It depends upon omens, chance, luck, supernatural miracles. . . . Spiritualism of the spirit, on the other hand, gives a man wholly to himself. It maketh him *free* indeed!"

In evaluation of this unusual man, Michael O'Shaughnessy said in *Andrew Jackson Davis—"Poughkeepsie Seer"*:

There is no doubt of Jackson's profound sincerity and self-belief. He never forgot his personal limitations and lack of education, and it is in his favor that he did not take pride in his basic ignorance. On the contrary, he managed to procure a degree in Medicine which he thought would give greater weight and authority to his healing abilities, rather than remain satisfied with his psychical dexterity. He gradually became the master of an extraordinary prose, which he wrote without spirit guidance. The reader becomes so enmeshed in fruity verbiage, so saturated in passages of purplest prose that it is clear he made up for his abstemiousness in other directions by phenomenal verbosity. But when Jackson goes into an inspired state it is another matter. There he expresses the views of Swedenborg in that philosopher's idiom, although only a few copies of Swedenborg's *The Economy of the Animal Kingdom* had just reached this country and could not have been read by Davis.

And it is written for all to see in his books that he predicted in detail motor cars and airplanes operating on a new kind of fuel, palatial railroad coaches on trains that would be advertised to give "through travel to California in four days." All of which was pretty supernormal for 1856.

Davis had numerous followers and caused a lot of controversy over a period of many years. During this time, magazines throughout America discussed mesmerism and magnetism, now more frequently being called hypnosis, with increasing regularity. Hypnotism had some champions with famous names in medicine and religion and also in politics. Such distinguished statesmen as Sam Houston, Daniel Webster, and Henry Clay expressed interest in it.

Aldred Scott Warthin was a nationally known pathologist and clinician, former editor of the *Annals of Clinical Medicine*, former president of the Association of American Physicians. Allan Angoff says: "He gave hypnosis a measure of respectability at a time when the magnetizers were still attracting wide-eyed audiences in a manner that still suggested circus barkers at sideshows and traveling medicine men without medical degrees or medical training. Surely, the final triumph of hypnosis as a therapy accepted by the conservative American Medical Association in June 1958 can be traced in some degree to the researches of such men as Aldred Warthin." This interesting man was born in Indiana in 1866 and had a distinguished career as a physician, naturalist, and musician. He was a botanist, a pianist with a diploma from the Cincinnati Conservatory of Music, a teacher of music who went on to earn a degree in medicine at the University of Michigan, after which he won another doctorate in philosophy, and taught pathology, clinical medicine, and medical history. This doctor, certainly the kind anyone would want to have on his side, did considerable experimentation with hypnosis, using music in his tests. He published the results in *Medical News*, but they did not attract any great amount of attention.

Another medical man who brought this study even more respectability was Dr. Morton Prince. His father, from a Back Bay family, had been elected mayor of Boston four times; his mother came from an equally distinguished Philadelphia family. Morton Prince received a bachelor's degree from Harvard College in 1875 and went on to Harvard Medical School, where he was graduated in 1879. When he studied overseas, it was undoubtedly his work with Dr. Charcot and at Nancy that aroused his lasting interest in hypnosis and other abnormal states of consciousness. He lectured on various aspects of neurology, human personality, and human behavior at many universities including Harvard, Tufts, London, Oxford, and Cambridge. He founded the *Journal of Abnormal Psychology* in 1906 and was the editor until his death in 1929.

And now we come to "the towering figure in American psychology and psychopathology, who saw more than therapy in hypnosis"—the great William James. He was America's "leading philosopher and psychologist, and, more important, a man unafraid to delve into the mysteries of the human psyche," to quote Angoff again. Born in New York City in 1842, James received a Doctor of Medicine degree from Harvard in 1870, and by the time he died in 1910 in New Hampshire,

he was the most famous and most daring psychologist in America, with honorary degrees from Padua, Princeton, Edinburgh and other universities. His *Principles of Psychology* (New York, 1890), *Pragmatism* (New York, 1907) and other works remain classic studies for the most orthodox and conventional students of human behavior, including those who would rather forget that he was a keen student of hypnosis and psychical research long before there was a degree of respectability in studying such phenomena soberly.

James was at one time president of the Society for Psychical Research, London, and was the chief instigator of the American Society for Psychical Research. He followed the British society in its initial investigations of hypnosis, and in a lecture before the Lowell Institute in Boston in 1896, he said: "Some minds would see a marvel in the simplest hypnosis—others would refuse to admit that there was anything new even if one rose from the dead. They would either deny the apparition, or say you could find a full explanation of it in Foster's *Physiology*."

All these great pioneering men would have agreed perfectly with lawyer Sydney L. Flower, the editor of *Suggestive Therapeutics*, when he said in 1889 that he abhorred the induction of hypnosis for purposes of amusement by the public exhibition of somnambulistic feats. . . . These entertainments are essentially vulgar. . . . There is a higher side to hypnotism which will never be admitted to full recognition as long as the charlatan is empowered to drag its name in the dirt. It is an agent for good; it is never, in skillful hands, an agency for evil. Its value to the physician and to the psychoanalyst cannot be estimated. It affords a means by which the power of the mind to heal the body may be manifested. Whether it be called . . . faith-healing, mental healing, osteopathy, massage, bone-setting, or suggestive therapeutics, the fact remains that the power itself is the power of the person cured to heal himself. Who shall name this power? Let it be the divine spirit, the soul, the subconscious—anything you will—it is these. I believe that hypnotism, rightly applied, is the most successful, because it can be the most universal method of calling this power into action!

8. Schemes of Self-Suggestion

"SUGGESTION FROM without must for the most part resolve itself into suggestion from within," wrote F. W. H.
Myers in *Human Personality and Its Survival of Bodily
Death*. But why it succeeds on some occasions and not others
is unknown. We cannot predict when the result will occur;
still less can we bring it about at our pleasure.

"Nay," goes on Myers, "we do not even know whether it
might not be possible to dispense altogether with suggestion
from the outside in most of the cases now treated in this way,
and merely to teach the patient to make the suggestions for
himself." No strong belief or enthusiasm is even necessary,
Myers discovered, and he quoted experimentation by Dr.
Hugh Wingfield (*Proceedings* S.P.R., Vol. V) to prove it.

Wingfield, a demonstrator in physiology at Cambridge
University, researched with a group of students who had had
no previous belief whatever in hypnosis. The phenomena of
self-suggestion occurred incidentally and quite unexpectedly

during a period of investigation on other points and were a surprise to everyone concerned. As a result, Wingfield's general thesis is: "It seems probable that . . . all phenomena capable of being produced by the suggestion of the hypnotizer can also be produced by self-suggestion in a self-suggestive subject."

All those who engaged in Wingfield's experiment were healthy young men between the ages of eighteen and twenty-four. It was presented to them that they attempt various things of a self-suggestive nature, and here are some of the curious results:

N. by means of stroking his arm and looking at it could render it rigid. He could not do so, however, if unable to see his arm.

Fi. could make his arm rigid by stroking only, whether or not he could see it.

F. could make his arm rigid by merely looking at it.

E. could make his arm rigid by an effort of mind without either seeing it or stroking it. His power of producing muscular rigidity was astonishing, for he was able by an effort of mind to throw his whole body into a state of cataleptic rigidity so that he could rest with his heels on one chair and head on another and remain supported in that condition.

Other unusual manifestations in the waking state were produced by this group using self-suggestion. T. and L. could both close their own eyes so that they were unable to open them. T. used to shut his eyes and stroke the lids downward. He was then unable to open them. Several other subjects showed the same ability. T. could fix his hand to the table by a few passes; this also was done by several others, and still others could fix their hands together.

The following experiment was tried: Five men were taken,

two of whom had been previously hypnotized; none were now sent to sleep. They were asked to put their hands together and imagine that they could not part them. They closed their eyes, put their hands together, and tried to part them. One could not part his hands; the others could. They were then told to shut their eyes and imagine the operator gazing at them and saying: "You cannot part your hands." Not one was able to separate them under those circumstances. These same phenomena could then be produced in themselves, quite apart from the operator, in their own rooms. They found at first that they were obliged to imagine the hypnotist giving the suggestion, but afterward were able to do it without visualizing him at all.

Wingfield added:

As regards delusions I can only give one instance. Doubtless many subjects could produce them in themselves if they tried, but I have never allowed them to do so. In the case of C., however, we have proof that they can be produced by self-suggestion. He could by a simple effort of mind make himself believe almost any delusion, e.g., that he was riding on horseback, that he was a dog or anything else, or that he saw snakes, etc. If left to himself the delusion vanished slowly. Anyone else could remove it at once by a counter-suggestion. He made these experiments without my consent, as I consider them unsafe.

It is interesting that while these tests were done in the latter part of the last century and then probably ignored or forgotten, today similar research is being undertaken. At the Medfield Foundation in Harding, Massachusetts, Dr. Theodore X. Barber has shown that four out of every five individuals are normally able to stay suspended between two chairs when they are simply asked to make their bodies rigid. Similarly, research conducted by John K. Collins at the University of Sydney in Australia has demonstrated that the average man or woman can remain suspended for up to four minutes. Absolutely no attempt was made to hypnotize these people. They were genuinely surprised at their own abilities, stating, for example: "I didn't know it could be so simple," and "I don't believe it; let me do it again."

An article in *Science Digest* (September 1969) by Richard F. Johnson entitled "Hypnosis: What it Can and Can't Do for You" states:

Dr. Martin T. Orne, formerly at Harvard and now at the University of Pennsylvania, has challenged the notion that hypnotism can produce a dramatic increase in strength. Nine men were exposed to a hypnotic induction procedure, given suggestions that they would not feel any fatigue, and then asked to hold a heavy weight at arms' length for as long as possible. Later, the same men were told, under normal conditions, that they were not performing better than women and that they would receive as much as $1.60 if they held the weight for a longer period of time. The men showed much greater strength and endurance, not under the hypnotic condition, but under the awake, motivated condition.

Johnson concludes his article with:

Within the scientific world, the main effect of this recent research has been a new interpretation of hypnosis. Hypnotism is now viewed as neither special nor mysterious. Man does not need the help of mythical forces in order to display unusual abilities such as great strength or high resistance to pain. His potential is simply much greater than he has allowed himself to believe.

It was similar ideas, occurring to Phineas Parkhurst Quimby, toward the middle of the last century that eventually led to the establishment of Christian Science. A prominent mesmerist, Quimby gave it up as a method of healing because he became convinced there was a psychical side to it. He decided, according to one of his students, Horatio W. Dresser, that:

The human mind is amenable to suggestion. . . . There are subjects capable of being put into a state which we now call hypnosis. . . . The alleged magnetic, electrical or mesmeric effects are not mysterious at all, but *are the results of the action of mind on mind.* . . . There is no such process as "mesmerism," therefore. There is no "magnetic healing." . . . There could be no mesmeric or magnetic science of healing, any more than there exists a medical science: the one true science is spiritual.

Quimby, says Allan Angoff, was a "strange and compelling pioneer" in the history of American healing. He was born in Lebanon, New Hampshire, in 1802, the son of a blacksmith, and, like Davis, he was a man of little schooling. Still, Ernest Sutherland Bates says of him in *The Dictionary of American Biography* that "among all the early American healers and eccentric philosophers his reputation stands the highest for beauty of character and honesty of purpose."

He began to work early as a clockmaker's apprentice and learned his craft eagerly and expertly. He married and became the father of four children. While working, he still apparently found time to read widely and, Angoff says, "finally came to his most absorbing interest, the human mind and its inexplicable powers." There is the possibility that he was led to this by his recovery from illness at an early age without the aid of medical science.

Quimby learned to hypnotize when he was thirty-six and became a professional mesmeric healer. He acquired as his subject a clairvoyant and clairaudient young man of nineteen, Lucius Burkmar, who when in a trance induced by Quimby diagnosed illnesses of the patients who came in increasing numbers. Then Quimby gave up clockmaking, toured New England with Lucius, and acquired a reputation as a healer and a man of utter honesty, being given the honorary title of "doctor" by scores of grateful patients he had cured when medicine had failed. He began to call his healing methods the Science of Christ, Christian Science, or Science of Health and Happiness, and he acquired a disciple who was eventually to become known to the world as Mary Baker Eddy, the founder of Christian Science.

Mary A. Morse Baker, afterward known as Mrs. Glover, Mrs. Patterson, and, finally, Mrs. Eddy because of her various marriages, was born at Bow, New Hampshire, on July 16, 1821, the youngest of six children of a farmer. She had childhood experiences such as many mediums do, of hearing voices calling her when no one was there. At the age of twenty-two she married for the first time, and six months later her husband died of yellow fever. A few months afterward a child was born, who was adopted by some neighbors. About ten years later she married again, a traveling dentist, and they lived together for some time, mostly in poverty, constantly moving from one place to another. They were divorced in 1873 on grounds of his desertion.

Before Patterson left Mary, he did her one big favor. He contacted Phineas Quimby for help for her multitudinous pains and aches. As often happens to a talented person who has not yet found his niche in life, she had endured much illness and had been practically bedridden for a long time with what was described as a spinal disease. During the following year she managed to get herself to the healer, so feeble that she had to be helped up the steps to his consulting room. She was worn and emaciated, shabbily dressed and extremely poor. All her adult life had been spent in poverty, and she had been a dependent invalid for nearly twenty years.

Mary Baker Whatsernames was a woman of great potential, but for forty years her life had been of the narrowest and barest kind. There had been no interests of wider scope into which she could pour her restless energies. But from the date she first saw Quimby all was changed. He not only restored her bodily health but gave her a purpose in life. Her enthusiasm for him and his teachings kept her occupied for years afterward. (It is said that when she was ill he was able to heal her telepathically at a distance.) At his death in 1866 she took over his philosophy as her own and continued to teach it, adding bits here and there to elaborate it into what has now become the large and powerful sect of Christian Science.

The first edition of *Science and Health with Key to the Scriptures* appeared in 1875; she married Mr. Eddy in 1877. "Of the bridegroom," wrote Podmore, "it is enough to say that he did what he was told. Mrs. Eddy told him the night before the marriage that she intended to marry him the next day and he obeyed. He died five years later." But by then Mrs. Eddy hardly needed him or anyone else. She was flocked around, revered, and almost worshiped by an ever increasing group of followers.

Oddly enough, in formulating her philosophical concepts she turned on hypnosis vehemently. Calling it animal magnetism, she inspired her followers with such a dread of it that they thought of it only as a vicious and harmful practice and do so to the present day. About Mr. Eddy's demise she said: "My husband's death was caused by malicious mesmerism.

. . . After a certain amount of mesmeric poison has been administered it cannot be averted. No power of mind can resist it."

By now she was also strongly against Spiritualism, although for a time after her first healing by Quimby she had been a professional medium, claiming that the spirit of her dead brother was her guide. Aside from these points of difference, her teachings were straight Quimby all the way. What had been revealed to him by his experiments with hypnosis—that the mind controls the body—was worked into a faith that, when used properly, kept her flock healthy and happy and often even wealthy. She brought members of her church healing and comfort, gave them a feeling of self-security and self-possession, and what more could anyone want?

Aside from going to church, hypnosis went on the stage during the last century, and it soon became a big star. No vaudeville bill was complete without an eerie mesmerist who put volunteers to sleep and then made them do foolish things. How the audiences laughed to see a man make love to an empty chair under the impression that a beautiful woman sat there or dance with an umbrella or crawl around on all fours barking like a dog. Today this sort of thing is just as popular in night club acts.

Michael Dean is an example of the better type proponent of this. Actually Dr. Sanford I. Berman, he holds a bachelor's degree from the University of Minnesota, a master's degree from Columbia University, and a Ph.D. from Northwestern. He told me he selected the challenge of becoming a stage hypnotist because he enjoys working with people, and his show provides him with the opportunity to illustrate dramatically the power of hypnosis in education and psychiatry.

It also brings in the dollars. One of his promotional brochures says: "Now You Too Can Learn How to be a Millionaire and discover the mental secrets of business success and personal effectiveness." The accent here is on the *too*. Dean admits that he has hit the million dollar mark in his chosen profession.

Michael Dean is billed as "the world's foremost hypnotist"; but Dr. Berman is billed as "one of the most popular lecturers on communication and semantics in the country." He took over classes in general semantics at the University of Chicago when Dr. S. I. Hayakawa went to San Francisco State—to become world renowned as the man who stood up against the hippie rebellion at his college. Dr. Berman has taught management and communication seminars and courses at Northwestern and the University of Chicago, he also teaches a course in communication at the University of California Extension in San Diego. He was recently elected to the Board of Directors of the International Society for General Semantics along with Dr. Hayakawa and Nicholas Johnson of the Federal Communications Commission.

Berman-Dean has several well-written and attractively printed booklets that he uses to teach his courses, and he is writing a hardcover book at the present time. As the world's foremost hypnotist, he has been breaking show business records at the Gaslight Supper Club in San Diego. He has also broken records for this sort of thing at the Sahara and Thunderbird hotels in Las Vegas and Harrah's clubs in Reno and Lake Tahoe. He is president of Revere Records and West Coast Productions. And he has put out a self-hypnosis record on which his magnetic voice helps one to get into a state of deep relaxation in which he can use his own mind to promote convictions of weight reduction, stopping smoking, improving memory, and so on. He also tours the country occasionally lecturing to business groups. Hundreds of businessmen in San Diego recently plunked down $10 for a three-hour lecture; and three hundred of them did it for four successive nights.

Dean uses his night club stage act to arouse interest in his courses, which are designed to aid people in learning self-hypnosis as a tool in everyday life. He terms hypnosis "a natural, perfectly safe mental function." By coupling hypnosis with general semantics, he feels he has a real key to personal and financial success for people willing to believe in themselves enough to give it a sincere try.

General semantics, Dean told Wayne Carpenter of the San Diego *Union*, is the process of defining the difference between words and things. "Words are merely symbols," the hypnotist says. "I try to show people fact on a non-verbal basis by teaching them how to communicate with themselves through hypnosis." His ultimate goal is to reveal how to teach people to deal with the "false symbols of our times and to live their lives on a scientific basis, regardless of their professional or educational level."

He believes it would be good for college students to undergo hypnosis regularly because it removes restrictive emotions of a student, thus eliminating problems he may have in study concentration and allowing him to use his full capacities in school.

"Hypnosis can be used as frequently as needed to improve grades, to break bad habits, or to stimulate one's love life," says Dean. He feels college instructors have special effects upon the thinking of thousands of students, and therefore "have a duty to educate students in the knowledge that hypnosis is not a mysterious power or magic or stage trick but a science." Students are warned that as a science, however, hypnosis should only be attempted by the knowledged professional who knows its dangers and effects.

"Hypnosis in the hands of a capable person is completely safe," Michael Dean maintains, "but if attempted by the unexperienced, the effects can be disastrous."

9. Rough Companions

SUCCESSFUL in the church and on the stage, hypnotism was now taken up by the authors, who, for a time, made the world "mesmerist" almost synonymous with glittering-eyed monsters.

In 1894 George Du Maurier published the novel *Trilby*, which became such a sensation that it gave a new word to the dictionary. "Svengali," you might say, *means* mesmerism to a great many people. In Du Maurier's story Trilby O'Ferrall, a lovely young girl, falls into the clutches of a hypnotist named Svengali, who is described as a "tall and bony character between thirty and forty-five, well-featured, but sinister." This well-featured but sinister entity "was very shabby and dirty, and wore a red beret and a large velveteen cloak. His thick, heavy, languid, lusterless black hair fell down behind his ears onto his shoulders. . . . He had bold, brilliant black eyes with long heavy lids, a thin sallow face, and a beard of burnt-up black which grew almost from his under eyelids, and over it his mustache, a shade lighter, fell in two long spiral twists."

After bending the beautiful Trilby to his will, Svengali makes a singer out of her, one so good that for five years she is known as "the first lady of the Continent." But she foils him by falling ill and dying, clearly showing that living five years under the spell of a Svengali is bad medicine.

Nathaniel Hawthorne, perhaps the greatest American novelist of his day, obviously believed in the Svengali image. When his wife wanted to use mesmerism to cure her headaches, he pleaded with her to "shun these magnetic miracles." He added: "I am unwilling that a power should be exercised on thee, of which we know neither the origin or the consequence. If I possessed such a power over thee, I should not dare to exercise it. . . . Supposing the power arises from the transfusion of one spirit into another, it seems to me that the sacredness of the individual is violated by it."

Martin Ebon, in his excellent work *They Knew the Unknown*, wrote that among authors of the time

"The Unknown" as ghost or mesmerist, or embodied in a man-made creature, reflected day-to-day fascinations and personal involvements. Mary Shelley did not invent Frankenstein in a vacuum. If it seems unlikely that a young, romantically inclined girl, traveling through Europe in the company of rich and brilliant poets, should have produced so morbid a piece of fiction, we must remember the bizarre interests of the Shelley circle. While Mary herself seems to have undergone few otherworldly experiences, her husband, Percy, recorded many pseudo-psychic phenomena in his hectic and short life. Once, when the Shelleys, Lord Byron, and Claire Clairmont—Mary's half-sister and Byron's mistress—were sitting by the fire telling ghost stories, Shelley suddenly experienced a panic, masquerading as x-ray clairvoyance: He thought he saw right through the young women's bodices, imagined their nipples staring at him, turning slowly into malevolent, jelly-like eyes. He leaped, screaming, from his chair and raced from the room.

Shelley sought several times to invoke psychic experiences by having himself hypnotized. Claire wrote in her journal on December 15, 1821, the year before his death, that Shelley had been magnetized. When he was, he begged them not to ask him any more questions because he would say what he ought not. Captain Thomas Medwin, a member of the eccentric Shelley circle, was probably his hypnotist, and his hypnosis experiences led to a discussion of the relation between soul and body. Shelley concluded that it had been proof of the soul's immortality.

One whose piercing eyes and mesmeric influence acquired him the reputation of a Svengali was Rasputin, who looked the role whether he deserved it or not. His daughter Maria insists he was a kindly man and a loving father, and there is just as much evidence for this in history as there is for his evil reputation. After all, he was a monk from the age of sixteen, he was beloved by the populace as a wandering preacher with healing powers, and he is said to have believed he was the reincarnation of Christ. So he could not have been all bad, and his history is fascinating.

Grigory Rasputin was born in the late 1860s (or 1871 according to the *Encyclopedia Britannica*) in Pokrovskoe, a small town near Tobolsk on the banks of the Tura in the steppes of Siberia. He was the son of relatively well-to-do parents, for his father, Yefimy Rasputin, was a coachman and owner of horses who worked hard and developed his land into a prosperous farm. (*Britannica* says his father was poor.) Rasputin had a happy childhood, loving the horses and the steppes, the swimming and the fishing—but not the discipline. Although his father taught him the rudiments of reading, he could see no point in learning to write, and even in adulthood his handwriting showed an awkward, childish scrawl.

Colin Wilson wrote in *Rasputin and the Fall of the Romanovs*:

From an early age, Grigory Rasputin had one curious characteristic that distinguished him from the other village boys; he possessed a degree of second sight. His daughter Maria quotes him as saying: "I never dared to steal or pilfer the smallest thing. I used to believe that everybody would at once see that I had stolen something, since I myself was aware of it as soon as one of my comrades had stolen. Even when he had stolen in a distant place and hidden the object, I could always see the object behind him." To illustrate his second sight, his daughter tells a story of St. Petersburg days, when an unknown woman called on Rasputin carrying a muff. As soon as she came in, Rasputin snatched at the muff, calling, "Drop that!" A revolver fell to the floor, and the woman collapsed in hysterics.

But Rasputin had one big failing. As he grew older he shocked the whole village with his sexual license, and he was to shock his tsar and country with it for the rest of his life. He never did anything by halves, and probably the naïve element of show-off that remained with him to the end encouraged him to acquire and keep the reputation of a rake. But Wilson wonders if he was invariably, or even usually, successful in his amours. "His methods were not refined, as many St. Petersburg ladies bore witness. If he liked a woman he would try and grab her and kiss her, and then proceed to undo her buttons." This is not always the most subtle approach.

All his life Rasputin loved to sing and dance. Visitors who went to see him in St. Petersburg at the height of his power record that he would be carried away by his own oratory about religion until he would suddenly burst into song and then begin to dance.

In his youth Rasputin married a young lady who had boundless admiration for her husband and a docile, yielding character. In 1890 came an event that changed the course of his life. His wife bore him a son he adored, but in six months the infant died. He was shattered and immediately decided to go to see the hermit Makary to ask him what the death meant. He spent much time brooding over the Scriptures and on his knees praying; he paid visits to several monasteries and began to acquire the reputation of a "God seeker."

Then one day in the spring he saw a strangely dressed vision of the Virgin hanging in the sky, beckoning to him with her hand. He set a cross at the place where he had seen her and returned home, inspired to somehow seek out what she had been trying to communicate to him. He set out on a pilgrimage with a friend, walked two thousand miles to Greece to visit Mount Athos, then on to the Holy Land, then another thousand miles across Turkey. On his way back home, in a cathedral in Kazan, he was startled to see an image of the Virgin dressed as she had appeared to him. Two years later he arrived home, greatly changed. His eyes had acquired a penetrating quality that made some of the peasants imagine he could see straight through them. Yes, he had discovered he had hypnotic powers as well as second sight. Even the members of his own village respected him and became his followers.

For some years after, he traveled most of the time, returning home only occasionally to provide his wife with another child. (Maria, who lives and lectures in this country—I have heard her defend her father vehemently—was born in 1898.) His reputation grew and grew as a prophet and a

clairvoyant and one who was capable of healing illnesses by
the laying on of hands. He was also notedly generous. Whenever gifts of money or valuables were given him, he immediately gave them away to the needy. Many regarded him as a
saint, except for his slight tendency to seduce women. His
attitude toward sex was pagan, and he did not count it a sin
to sleep with some of his admiring converts. In fact, there is
one theory that it was actually part of his religion. Those
who went to him expecting a sermon were sometimes discon-
certed when he pressed their bosoms to his bosom and suggested they remove some of their clothing. But if they were
nervous he might revert immediately to the role of a spiritual
adviser apparently incapable of lust. It was always difficult,
even from those earliest days, to know whether he was a saint
or a devil.

By 1900 Rasputin, approaching his middle thirties, was
famous in Siberia and well on his way toward St. Petersburg
and eternal fame—or infamy. Despite his intelligence,
strength, and immense nervous force, he was basically an
ordinary superstitious Russian peasant. He was a broad
shouldered man, not as tall as he is usually depicted, with a
thin and straggly brown beard, and piercingly hypnotic blue-
gray eyes. His manner was cheerful, overflowing with benev-
olent vitality, his expression habitually good natured; and he
modulated his voice like an actor, with ease of manner and
charm. He was persuasive and compelling, and it was said
that he had healed a paralyzed man merely by ordering him
to stand up.

The Grand Duchesses Militza and Anastasia, the daughters of King Nikita of Montenegro (now Yugoslavia), introduced him at court. Like most others in high society in Russia, they were interested in religion, magic, mysticism,
Spiritualism, and table rappings, and no doubt had heard

much that was interesting about this new healer from Siberia.

In *Rasputin, a New Judgement,* Heinz Liepman offers a completely different account of how it all came about. He suggests that Rasputin had been noticed by the secret police and that Prince Pirakov, one of the leaders of the Union of True Russians, decided he might be used to counteract the influence of various fakers, frauds, and miracle workers at court. He does not, however, explain how Rasputin came to the attention of Prince Pirakov.

Tsar Nicholas Romanov was loved by no one but his family. He was the gentlest, most pleasant and most charming of men, but he was vascillating and yielding, with no sense of reality. On top of this he had a strong streak of stubbornness. He had been wisely determined about only one thing, his love for Princess Alice of Hesse, a granddaughter of Queen Victoria. She was shy, gentle, sad, and awkward socially, and it may have been because both she and Nicholas were so unsure of themselves that they were drawn together. Their marriage was entirely successful, and they never ceased to love each other; but their relations toward other people were always unproductive.

Alexandra was prolific with daughters. She had four before an heir to the throne finally arrived, and then he had hemophilia! Naturally she coddled him to the point of hysterical mania.

It is difficult to be sympathetic toward this royal couple because of their personalities and also because of a few of Nicholas' traits that were not entirely likable. It is reported that when his soldiers shot down unarmed workers he commented: "Fine fellows!" and when told that 150 peasants had been killed and 200 wounded on Bloody Sunday he said: "Are you sure you've killed enough?" He lost me right there.

So these were the kinds of people our sexy, gutsy Rasputin got mixed up with. In a short time after he arrived in St. Petersburg his reputation as a miracle worker was established by local healings, and crowds assembled at his home, waiting two or three days before being able to approach him. When the little tsarevitch became ill with a high fever, Rasputin was sent for. After he had prayed for the boy, he said: "Your son, little mother, is now sleeping peacefully." Later that night Nicholas wrote in his diary: "Made the acquaintance of a man of God, Grigory from Tobolsk province. Alexei was saved from certain death by his prayers."

From then on Rasputin was almost like one of the family. There was bound to be gossip about the tsarina and him, but with Alexandra's devotion to her husband it is difficult to believe that there was anything to it. Yet here is a most suspicious letter to him from her. We have to evaluate it according to our own reactions. (I know what I think.)

My beloved unforgettable teacher, redeemer and mentor! How tiresome it is without you! My soul is quiet and I relax only when you, my teacher, are sitting beside me. I kiss your hands and lean my head on your blessed shoulders. Oh, how light, how light do I feel then! I only wish one thing: to fall asleep, to fall asleep forever on your shoulders and in your arms. What happiness to feel your presence near me. Where are you? Where have you gone? Come quickly, I am waiting for you and I am tormenting myself for you. . . . I love you forever!

Well, be that as it may, Rasputin kept healing the boy whenever he received an injury that caused bleeding, so the tsar had to have him nearby. And also, it must be admitted that his vitality recharged this dull couple.

Even Prince Yussupov, the man who eventually killed

Rasputin, confessed that he was a hypnotist of great talent. In *Rasputin, His Malignant Influence and His Assassination* he wrote of a healing session he had with him:

His hypnotic power was immense. I felt it subduing me and diffusing warmth throughout the whole of my being. I grew numb; my body seemed paralyzed. I tried to speak, but my tongue would not obey me, and I seemed to be falling asleep, as if under the influence of a strong narcotic. Yet Rasputin's eyes shone before me like a kind of phosphorescent light. From them came two rays that flowed into each other and merged into a glowing circle.

. . .

Such was my condition as I lay motionless, unable to call out or stir. Yet my mind was still free, and I realized that I was gradually falling into the powers of this mysterious man.

A slightly different description was given by one Vera Shukovskaya who said: "He pulled me into the bedroom and tore off my dress as we went. And the next moment he was nothing but savage animal desire. The last thing I remember is his tearing off my underclothing, then I lost consciousness. I awoke and found myself lying on the ground, torn and defiled."

But this was the lady's second visit. Why had she returned to him? It was his hypnotic power that drew her back. "Certain men seem to be born already in touch with the 'inner power-house'," she said.

When Rasputin came to St. Petersburg he knew little of politics, and he disliked intrigue. Yet within five years, without fully intending it, he was the center of all the intrigue in the city. He had many enemies; so did the tsar. The government was a mess, and it was to get worse.

Rasputin still kept his appearance picturesquely casual,

but he took care not to be personally offensive. The tsarina and her daughters, of whom he was a pet, gave him embroidered blouses and shirts, and other admirers gave him velvet trousers and patent leather boots. He became almost a dandy, even on occasion using scent. He was happy to accept presents of clothing and wine and such things, but he gave away money as fast as he received it. Yet his manners became steadily worse, and he was incredibly insolent. He made it a point to humiliate the high and mighty of both sexes. Had luxurious living and heavy drinking softened his brain? Even his friends felt he was going too far. No wonder he came to be called the most unpopular man in Russia.

Then when drunk at parties he began to speak familiarly (and thus disrespectfully—it was the same thing) of the tsar, and the word got back to his majesty. So by 1915 he was no longer welcome at the palace, and the tsarina had to meet him secretly. The First World War was going on at the time, and people even suggested that Rasputin and the empress were conspiring together as German spies!

Then Nicholas went to the front, leaving his wife in charge of the country—and naturally she turned to her mentor for constant advice. It was during this time that Prince Yussupov decided he had to kill Rasputin. The Mad Monk had always known people wanted to kill him. Now he suddenly knew for sure when it would be. He wrote a letter predicting it and also giving his thoughts about the situation of the country and the tsar: "If I'm killed by peasants, all will be well with the country, if killed by the nobility, for twenty-five years there will be no nobles in the country. None of the Tsar's family will remain alive for more than two years. I shall be killed."

Yussupov invited Rasputin to a midnight meeting, gave

him poisoned cake and wine—and nothing happened. Yussupov then shot Rasputin in the back, but he later stood up and then crawled up the steps on all fours. He came to a locked door and with tremendous strength, burst it open. Two more shots hit him, and he collapsed. Then he was taken to the river and pushed through a hole in the ice. He was still even then enough alive to manage to make the sign of the Cross with one hand.

We all know what happened after that. Lenin came back from exile; the royal family was kept prisoner in the palace at Tsarskoe Selo; and then they were taken to Ekaterinburg and murdered.

And so ended the career of a remarkable man who had many unusual talents, and a few unusual vices. Colin Wilson wrote:

Rasputin is a great deal more interesting than any of his biographers seem to have realized. His real significance may not be recognized for at least another century—by which time, one hopes, psychical research, telepathy, second-sight and pre-vision will be accepted as simply another branch of psychology. Possibly the word "abnormal" will have somewhat changed its connotations by then.

10. Mrs. Z—and Her ESP

WHILE A HYPNOTIST was causing disruption in Russia, another was performing a constructive scientific investigation in Mexico. Dr. Gustav Pagenstecher, a German physician practicing in Mexico City, had discovered a somnambulic patient who could produce psychometry when in trance. He studied and recorded her information so carefully that exact accounts of many very unusual phenomena are available.

Psychometry is a form of ESP explained by the premise that objects, or possibly the force fields around them, retain data. Today the phrase "token object test" is often substituted for psychometry in order to avoid confusion, because the word has other definitions in other disciplines. In the usual kind of token object experiment, the subject tries to obtain ESP impressions about past events by means of objects that were associated with the event. It is possible for a good medium to "read" a watch or earring or shoe and give considerable information about its owner, which he has no normal way of knowing.

Pagenstecher was born in Germany in 1855 and received his medical degree from the University of Leipzig. Shortly afterward he left for Mexico, which was his home until he died in 1942. It was no rash youngster, therefore, who, when he discovered the talented patient, threw himself into the uncertain area of psychical research, but a man in his sixties who was a respected member of the medical profession.

Pagenstecher said he had been a materialist for forty years when he had his first encounter with the paranormal, but he was to change his opinions radically after working with Mrs. Z——. He was not too conventional a physician to begin with though, for he did not hesitate to use hypnotic therapy in his treatment of the patient, whose insomnia led her to him for help. This was still only 1918, remember.

Señora María Reyes de Z—— (Mrs. Zierold) was identified primarily as Mrs. Z—— in the reports Dr. Pagenstecher wrote about her. She was obviously a woman of remarkable natural psychic gifts, and hypnosis brought them out. The doctor first became aware of them while treating her for her sleeplessness, from which she suffered severely as a result of a stomach ulcer and then as an aftereffect of the operation. It was when drugs failed to relieve her that hypnosis was tried.

During one of the early sessions, Mrs. Z—— was disturbed by the impression that her fifteen-year-old daughter was eavesdropping outside the door. When this was checked, it was found to be true. Until that time, Mrs. Zierold was unaware of possessing any psychic abilities. Her ESP developed gradually after that during the course of a hypnotic training program instigated by the doctor.

There is an interesting account written by Mrs. Zierold about the growth of her gifts by the procedure Pagenstecher evolved, which was designed to help her learn to visualize.

At first he instructed her to try to "see" him in various parts of the room, although he was actually out of her sight. She did this, and there was a gradual development of clarity in her mental pictures. Mrs. Z— writes: "I began to see, upon order, first a kind of shadow corresponding to the body of the doctor; later on I was able to see him with absolute clearness, whether I was blindfolded or not, and whether he was standing in front of me or at my back, or even behind the door, as it happened several times."

From the beginning of research in parapsychology, many investigators have been of the opinion that hypnosis, sleep, or other forms of dissociation or altered states of consciousness are necessary to produce ESP. We will see a little later how Dr. Milan Ryzl trained his subjects to achieve such states. Pagenstecher, however, was the first investigator to use hypnosis as a means of cultivating ESP in a gifted subject. Although others before him had conducted tests that would reveal traveling clairvoyance or other talents in hypnotized subjects, no one had systematically utilized the trance state as a means to *develop* the subject's mental images.

With the lady's consent, the doctor embarked on a series of experiments designed to test whether the blocking of her physical senses by hypnosis in some way stimulated her paranormal perception. He found that when, in response to his suggestion, she was impervious to the pain of needle thrusts, unresponsive to loud noises in her ears or to the sharp smell of ammonia, she would nevertheless report accurately sensations of vision, smell, taste, hearing, and feeling received from objects unknown to her that were placed in her fingers. Although the purpose of the experiments was first thus to test her extrasensory perception, Pagenstecher was further surprised to find Mrs. Z—— reporting details connected with the history of background of these objects.

When the doctor realized that she could give this information seemingly related to the past histories of objects she held in her hands, he worked out a system in order to test her in the most scientific manner possible. In his experiments, anything she said regarding the experimental object counted as a response, the target range being limited only by its past history. She continued to operate in the trance state and did not, as far as is known, show evidence of ESP unless she was hypnotized.

Risking his considerable reputation as a physician, Pagenstecher, in 1919, a few months after he began his experiments, reported on them to the medical society of Mexico City, of which he was a member. He asked the society to appoint a committee to study Mrs. Z—— in trance, and the society cooperated. Several pumice stones were used in the experiments for the committee. They had been chemically treated, although there were no odors or other distinguishing characteristics among them. Then Mrs. Zierold described the lake from which four of the stones had come, reported strong odors from those that had been soaked in chemicals, received the sensation of heat from one that had been heated for a short time several days previously, sensations of cold from another that had been subjected to low temperatures, and even noted the "tick-tock of a clock and the sound of church bells" when she held a stone that had earlier been placed for a period in the case of a striking clock. The medical committee upheld Pagenstecher's claim that the phenomena were indeed of a supernormal nature.

In 1921 the doctor reported his experiments to the American Society for Psychical Research, and Dr. Walter Franklin

Prince went to Mexico to check his results. Prince had been an Episcopal minister until he became so interested in psychical phenomena that he began to work with the ASPR as its principal research officer. For many years he was one of America's most outstanding figures in the field.

Prince was in his late fifties when he visited Mexico in 1921. He had two traits essential for an investigator: He was open-minded about the possible range of facts in nature, and he was hard-headed in their appraisal. Both traits are conspicuous in his accounts of his experiences in Mexico. Being well-known for his exposures of fraudulent mediums red-handed, he arrived in Mexico with a similar object in view. He was soon to be convinced otherwise.

An example of the kind of testing Dr. Prince did with Mrs. Z— follows:

The experimental objects were three pieces of paper from a pad belonging to a colleague of Pagenstecher's who had suffered a stroke. On the first piece of paper presented to Mrs. Zierold the stricken doctor had written a call for medical help with his left hand, since he had lost the use of his right hand and also could not speak. The note on the second piece of paper was written shortly before, at the onset of the stroke, with the right hand, while he could still use it. Finally, the third piece, taken from the bottom of the pad, had presumably not been touched by the doctor. Señora de Z— had the following impressions when she held the first piece of paper:

I am in an office, sitting on a desk, in front of a man whose face has a bluish tint, whose eyes are languid and whose mouth is slightly distorted. He tries to write something with his left hand which apparently contains an order, as an elderly lady who is at his side with two other . . . women leaves the room hurriedly and comes back with another woman. In the meantime, a young man of about thirty-five years of age has unfastened the collar of the sick man and gives him some water to drink. At his side stands a young girl of about sixteen or eighteen years who pets him and kisses him very affectionately. After some time a man of vigorous constitution enters the room and receives from the left hand of the sick man a small instrument which had been extracted by him from a pocket instrument case [a small lancet for bleeding]. Aided by the newcomer [the doctor called for] the young man already mentioned lifts up the invalid and carries him out of the room into an adjoining room, while I keep on seated upon the desk, being unable to move.

These impressions were correct. The doctor had suddenly been taken ill with a stroke, and the other events followed as described. In response to the second sheet of paper, she said: "I do not understand what I see. It seems to me there are *two conflicting visions,* superimposed one on top of the other and blending together." The first impression:

"I see a large room, small boys with caps on their heads who push wheel carts filled with scraps of paper of different colors and also with old rags. I see women who separate the different colors with long forks. The scraps and pieces of rags are thrown into a large boiler."

Mrs. Zierold's second impression from that sheet of paper was:

"I see a very sick man, with bluish face, who tries to speak without results as I see only the movement of his lips and do not hear a word. He takes a pencil with his right hand and writes something on a blank paper."

Finally, the third sheet—the one from the bottom of the pad—produced only more images from the paper factory.

Not surprisingly, the responses that concerned vivid or emotionally intense events were the most convincing from the point of view of supplying evidence for ESP. Several contained detailed descriptions, such as the one concerning the doctor, that it seemed impossible that Mrs. Z—— could have produced by normal means. It is emphasized by both the investigators that the subject did not examine the experimental object either by sight or by touch. Once her fingers came in contact with it, she did not move them for the duration of the test. In fact, she entered a cataleptic trance as soon as she received the object, and it lasted until the end of the session. In several instances, the events described by Mrs. Z—— and later found to have been associated with the object could not have been rationally inferred even if she had examined it.

On another occasion she was given a string to which the identification plate belonging to a German ex-sergeant had been attached, which had been worn by him during the First World War. Pagenstecher knew this about the string, but nothing more. Mrs. Zierold, of course, had not been told anything. When hypnotized she said:

It is intensely cold and the day is foggy. . . . I am on a battlefield; it smells of gunpowder. In front of me I see a tall man standing, with a big gray overcoat on, which reaches to his feet. Behind him I see three other men standing likewise. They talk German, or better said, they shout. In front of them and lying on the snow, behind an earthwork, I see a line of soldiers keeping up a continuous rifle fire. Some five meters back of the firing line there are two groups of men plainly to be seen, one consisting of about five to six men, and another one of about twelve to fifteen men. Quite of a sudden I see coming through the air and moving with great rapidity a big red ball of fire . . . which drops just in the midst of the fifteen men, tearing them to pieces. Arms, legs, heads, pieces of uniform fly through the air. I hear the dreadful yell of the wounded and the piteous moaning of the dying. This is a terrible sight.

Sergeant Saenger stated in response to this that on a cold and foggy morning on the Russian Front during World War I, he was with his superior officer ("a tall, solidly built man . . . wrapped in a large gray mantle") and two other noncommissioned officers, making four with himself, when an incendiary shell exploded on a barn housing a section of rapid fire guns and killed twenty-five soldiers who were there.

"This fire bomb," Saenger said, "was the only one to hit the mark in those days, and on account of the terrible sight I witnessed, when seeing the building aflame and hearing the distressing yells of dear friends buried under the burning debris, I am certain that this was the first great impression I received of the war, possibly the greatest of all, as it happened to be in the first month of my life as a soldier."

W. G. Roll, director of the Psychical Research Foundation and perhaps the best authority on the Pagenstecher case, stated in "Pagenstecher's Contribution to Parapsychology":

When Prince became convinced that the results were not to be explained in terms of cheating or some other normal explanation, he turned to the telepathic hypothesis, e.g., to the theory that Mrs. Z. responded to information about the experimental object in the minds of the experimenters rather than to any unknown properties inherent in the object itself. Prince gave up the telepathic hypothesis when he found that it made no difference to Mrs. Zierold what information, if any, the experimenters had about the object. Prince was co-experimenter on two occasions when Mrs. Zierold's statements about the experimental object were in conflict with his own opinions and when he thought she had failed in the test. In both cases it turned out that it was he and not Mrs. Zierold who was mistaken. He concluded from this that she was not reading his mind. In addition, there were cases where no one present had the information that Mrs. Zierold produced, such as the Ramón case.

It was shortly after Dr. Prince arrived that Mrs. Z——'s most dramatic test of all was given her, and she passed with flying colors. Pagenstecher had received a letter from a friend who had heard of her gift and hoped it could be used to give peace of mind to a friend of his. This was to be the famous Ramón case.

Mrs. Zierold was hypnotized and then given a small paper folded and secured with several wax seals. Her hands almost immediately became rigid and remained so throughout the trance. Then she began to speak of being on a ship where there were many frightened people. She described rapidly and excitedly a tall, stout, fair-skinned Spanish gentleman with black hair and eyes, full beard and mustache, and a large scar over his left eyebrow. (She was later to change this to right eyebrow.)

"Now he tears out a leaf from a little book, he turns to write . . . against the wall," she said.

Then there was an explosion and much confusion, life-savers being donned, screaming and weeping being heard. The man wrote more on the paper, rolled it up, and put it in a bottle. He drove in the cork by pounding it against the wall and then threw the bottle overboard.

Señora de Z—— gave several terrified screams. She gasped and said; "I'm drowning!" She was suffering, so she was quickly brought out of trance, but she continued to tremble all over, saying; "They're all drowned!" She remembered her vision and now repeated it with many more details.

When the seals were broken on the note she had held in her hand, the penciled message was found to read: "The ship is sinking. Goodbye, my Luisa, take care that my children do not forget me. Your Ramón." The lines were written straight, then the following was added in steeply slanting lines: "Havana. May God protect you and me also. Goodbye."

The story behind all this was that Ramón P—— was a Spanish political refugee staying in Cuba with his wife and brother and two children. He had been to New York on business and had then announced in his last letter to his wife his intention to start for Europe, even though those were the days when a great many ships were being sunk by the Germans. It was not known what ship he sailed on, but it was presumed he had embarked under an assumed name for political reasons. It was very likely he had been on the *Lusitania,* which was sunk at precisely the time that Ramón was missing.

After a year the note had been delivered to Ramón's widow, having been found in a bottle washed up on the shore.

Mrs. Zierold's description of Ramón was so accurate that it set his wife's anxieties about the death of her husband at rest. Having her own suspicions so thoroughly confirmed about the possible reason for his disappearance no doubt put her mind at ease—at least somewhat.

11. Mediumship

HAD MRS. ZIEROLD CONTINUED with the psychic development that began with her somnambulistic reading of token objects, she might have become one of the world's famous mediums, with the head start she had. Many sensitives begin their development by first being hypnotized. The late Eileen J. Garrett discovered how to do this for herself when she was but a girl. We are fortunate to have her statement about her thinking along these lines, and especially her comparison of the various forms of trance.

In a *Tomorrow* article entitled "Roads to Greater Reality" Mrs. Garrett said:

In my own case, which has included experiences in self-hypnosis as well as hypnosis under medical supervision, many years were spent in activities involving mediumistic trance, both inside and outside laboratory settings. Despite these years of experience, I cannot be dogmatic about these different states of mind. I can simply state my own reactions—how it feels to be the subject, to be on the "inside" of self-hypnosis, hypnosis and mediumistic trance.

Mrs. Garrett began auto-hypnotic trance as part of an innocent release process in her childhood.

Perhaps a desire to escape plays a part, having its origin in the daydreaming and imaginary play of a child who had few close playmates. Later in life, self-hypnosis developed to a point where it became identified with amnesia. Eventually it grew into a means for perceiving and receiving information from the living—clairvoyantly, telepathically—and apparently from the dead, through mediumship.

First, then, what does she mean by self-hypnosis?

It is withdrawal from the conscious self into an area of the nonconscious self, where the objective mind can no longer invent nor predict activity. And yet, within this other mind, life is being worked out on a different level—a level not particularly identified with others, nor with the self as such, but a place within, an inner world, where a battery of symbols takes over its own area of rhythmic sound and color.

Today, in order to place myself in an auto-hypnotic trance, I begin by suggesting to myself that I am withdrawing from the world of reality. In a moment I close my eyes to the external world. I am no longer listening or taking note of anything. I am going within, within, and within.

This is more or less an automatic process. Gradually I begin to feel a sense of excitement in the lower areas of the body. As though I had pulled a lever in the mind, a change in perceptiveness enables me to listen to myself speak. And I am speaking from a region that is more basic and authoritative, so it automatically seems to me to sound more definite than if I were speaking with my eyes open.

I then slow down the speaking process, until the time comes

that I withdraw deeper and further away, into a stage of absolute quiet, where I know that everything in the mind will really cease to be of any particular importance.

Then comes that moment when I have finished shifting gears. I become aware that I now have to produce, as it were, a new method of breathing. Eventually I will want to take more oxygen and I will yawn the conscious mind out of existence and begin to operate on another level.

In the auto-hypnotic trance, Mrs. Garrett says there is a sense of travel, of getting away from everything.

On the other hand, when placed under hypnosis by the physician, I am always peculiarly mentally alert. I am listening to what he tells me; at the same time, I am telling myself that I must be in contact with him on another level, so that I will be ready, anxious and willing to obey.

Nevertheless, as he talks to me I am fast losing active consciousness and I am setting up, as it were, two gateways: one through which his words may reach me all the time; and another, through which my own mind will not function. So, working with a hypnotist gives me a much more restricted area than I have when I work auto-hypnotically.

The mediumistic trance, on the other hand, utilizes more than just the normally automatic consciousness that operates through known senses. It calls upon an additional consciousness, seems to insist on examining, taking in everything, even though it may not be comprehended.

In a way Mrs. Garrett helps to explain how it is that so much can be given by those who have been hypnotically regressed, ostensibly into past lives, when she says:

Now, when we let the idea of the consciousness emerge, it displays so much energy, it has so much more "life," so much more to give of energy, that there is the tendency for internal drama to be personified, that the inner excitement may show itself through all kinds of histrionics that are difficult to discipline. The mind, released from what we would call the ordinary "normal" way of our thinking, is frisking about like a young dog, ready to fetch and carry all kinds of the most exciting bits of stuff that it finds on the way.

Our minds, like the atmosphere, would seem to be loaded with bits and pieces of thought or fact. We are like birds, going out to gather oddments from which to make what we might call "the nest of the mind." This process goes on, whether under auto-hypnosis or hypnosis from the outside. The essential difference is that, under hypnosis, I am subject to the doctor-hypnotist's wish and will, as soon as a condition of empathy has been established.

Auto-hypnosis, on the other hand, places me under my own suggestion. In a sense, it permits me to roam more widely. But this is largely a matter of degree. In both instances, the same reactions and mechanisms are at work. Indeed, in self-hypnosis, I will address myself as would an outsider, saying, "Eileen, you will now slowly relax, you will grow more passive, etc."

Hypnosis or self-hypnosis therefore must function, not as means of escape or self-dramatization, but as roads to a fuller understanding of the existence in which man dwells. Such deeper knowledge may help us to enrich and renew the devastated life that makes up today's civilization.

Another great medium, Britain's Douglas Johnson, has also written on "The Mechanics of Mediumship" (*Light*, Summer 1969). He says:

I find that when I am hypnotized (and I have done quite a lot of work under deep hypnosis), I've got powers that I did not know I had. I have described in detail the contents of an envelope, for example, for researchers, with an accuracy that is not possible when I am not hypnotized. Does hypnosis reactivate, or increase something within the medium? I think it does remove certain critical faculties in oneself. In mediumship it is very difficult to say something that may seem ridiculous (to a meeting or someone who is consulting you), and, of course, under hypnosis you have to say everything. I find being in a hypnotic trance is extremely relaxing psychically; somehow or other you are completely at peace, and it seems to come more easily.

Ordinary trance can vary very much in depth. People can be excellent trance mediums and hear the whole lot, and it can be rather like a sort of dream. With me, I might, when in trance, hear the first part, and then not hear, and then at the end begin to hear again. In such a case, unless somebody said to me afterwards, "Oh, yes, you said such and such a thing," then it would be like trying to bring back a dream that you've had. (There are also, of course, rarer cataleptic states of trance.) At one time I did almost all my appointments in trance, but now I find I can get exactly the same results by working normally, which is far less tiring.

Industrialist David Kahn met the famous Virginia Beach Seer when he was just a boy, and they became lifelong friends. In *My Life with Edgar Cayce* (as told to Will Oursler) Kahn detailed how Cayce went into hypnotic trance. They first met because the then young psychic had been invited to Lexington, Kentucky, to heal Mrs. DeLaney, Kahn's next-door neighbor.

At his own request Cayce had been told nothing about the patient beforehand. When he walked into the house Mr. De-Laney asked him if he wanted to see Mrs. DeLaney; but he said no, he preferred not to at that time. He would meet her after he gave the reading about her, and then he could see how closely his impression fit the reading.

Kahn said: "I noticed that once or twice he said 'we' instead of 'I.' Some time later, I asked him why he did this. Cayce said, 'I—and the forces that give me this power—we work together.' "

Cayce told Kahn that by himself he did nothing; he was simply a channel by which and through which the information flowed. That first day, before the reading, he gave Kahn a black book with some suggestions neatly typed in it, which Dave was to give him at the proper time. He said he would lie on his back, with his hands placed across his abdomen and his feet close together and he would look at the ceiling. Dave was then to say to him: "Now, Mr. Cayce, you are going to sleep . . ." and the rest of the material that was typed in the book. Then when Cayce said the words that would come at the end: "I am through . . . ready for questions" Kahn would ask for any questions that Mr. DeLaney or his doctor felt they wanted answered.

The typing in the black book consisted of suggestions for putting the seer into a hypnotic sleep, in which he could absolutely sever himself from his conscious mind and would have no awareness of his own words. After telling him that he was to go to sleep, Kahn would say: "You will hear me and follow the suggestions that I make to you. Answer slowly and distinctly because I am writing in longhand." After this Dave followed his instructions by saying: "Mr. Cayce, you are now at 58 Hampton Court in Apartment 1-A, in Lexington, Kentucky. Present in this room are Mr. William De-Laney, and Mrs. DeLaney's physician, and David E. Kahn. You will allow your mind to go to the rear of the apartment and there you will locate Mrs. DeLaney. When you have found her body you will go over it in great detail. Tell us any physical condition you find that might need correction."

Kahn says:

I was, of course, a neophyte at this kind of thing. I followed his instructions precisely, giving the first suggestion just as his eyes were about to close. If the person giving the instructions waited even a few seconds beyond this point to give the order, Cayce would go into a natural sleep but would not be able to speak or answer questions. Fundamentally, although there were minor changes and additions, the form of suggestion we used then was never changed in all the years and thousands of readings that followed.

After the order was given to go to the back of the apartment, Mr. Cayce in the living room said: "Yes, we have the body and mind of Mrs. DeLaney here." He proceeded then to go over her like a doctor, giving blood pressure and blood count and other physiological details. He said she was a paralytic and described her condition in medical terminology. Then he recommended an osteopath and gave his name and prescriptions for several medications for her to take internally.

After he had answered the questions put to him, he said: "We are through for the present." Then Kahn said: "Now, Mr. Cayce, you've given an excellent description of Mrs. DeLaney's condition. Thoroughly relaxed and perfectly refreshed, without any ill effects of any kind from the condition of the patient whom you have discussed, within three minutes you will wake up."

The woman who had this reading took the prescriptions given her and used them as stated. She was soon so much improved that she could drive her car, looking radiant, and could get around on her own.

This is the way it was at the beginning, and the way it continued all through Cayce's life—and David Kahn's. He was never to waver in his enthusiasm for his mentor and in his faithfulness to him. By following his readings, he had a successful, prosperous and happy life.

Edgar Cayce kept his own family in good shape also. His son Edgar Evans Cayce told about this in "Miracles were my Father's Business" (*Fate*, May 1960). He wrote:

When the family lived in Selma, Alabama, where Father had his photo studio, there was a terrible accident. My older brother, Hugh Lynn, had exploded a whole tray of flash powder in his face. The doctors said he'd be blind for life, at least in one eye. One proposed that the worst damaged eye be removed in hopes of saving the other one. Hugh Lynn . . . begged for a reading. Father's sleeping voice prescribed a poultice which a local pharmacist who believed in Father had made up and they used it.

Hugh Lynn's eyesight became perfect and he had hardly a trace of a scar.

"Mother's sickness," said Edgar Evans, "before I was born had been just as grave. It was tuberculosis, too far advanced for a cure before it was detected, so they said. A reading described a course of treatment and she recovered completely. At different times both my parents had had appendicitis. Readings told one to have an operation and the other not to—and both had enjoyed full and final recovery."

Edgar Evans was not to escape his father's ministrations either. In 1926 he stood too close to the fireplace. "There was a sudden wave of pain, flames curling around my legs, and someone screamed and screamed. It didn't seem to be me—but it was."

The boy would not let anyone touch him. All he wanted was for his father to read for him and find out what to do. So Cayce had himself put into his hypnotic trance and read for his injured son, prescribing cooling, healing dressings that were to perform a cure. Edgar Evans still has some of the scars; but his critically burned left leg was not too impaired for him to play football, baseball, and basketball in high school and tennis in college.

Incidentally, the son notes: "The faculty which Father took the greatest pains to conceal from everyone but Mother was his occasional ability to see people who weren't visible to others. He had experienced this phenomenon since early childhood and felt it branded him as a freak."

Swedish engineer Olof Jonsson of Chicago is one of the psychics who collaborated on telepathy experiments from outer space with Astronaut Edgar Mitchell of Apollo 14. He is, according to claims made by Brad Steiger in *The Psychic Feats of Olof Jonsson*, a telepathist, clairvoyant, and hypnotic healer.

On certain occasions, Olof Jonsson says he has placed people into hypnotic trance without even being near them or letting them know about his intentions—the good old telepathy at a distance we've already heard a bit about.

Steiger wrote: "Once at a party in Varberg, Sweden, Olof was challenged to undertake hypnotic experiments without being present in the same room as his subject and without having any personal contact whatsoever with the subject. Jonsson agreed, and the hostess suggested that the subject be a woman who had not yet arrived at the party." She had already expressed herself as willing to try hypnosis.

So two doctors, Mikkelson and Fardahl, agreed to control the experiment, and when Mrs. Bjerke arrived Olof immediately disappeared into the kitchen. There were then two rooms and two doors between his subject and him.

"When the lady sits in that armchair in front of the drapes," he had told the guests prior to Mrs. Bjerke's advent,

"I'll guarantee that she will fall asleep within two seconds."

It was about twenty minutes later when Mrs. Bjerke rang the doorbell. Olof immediately left the room. After the lady exchanged greetings with everyone present, she was shown to the armchair in front of the drapes. She had barely sat down before her head fell forward on her breast and she was sleeping quietly. The two doctors approached her, felt her pulse, lifted her head to be certain her sleep was sound, and tried to rouse her. They were unable to do so.

Then Olof was brought back into the room. He walked directly to the entranced woman and stood before her. "You are calm and composed," he told her. "It was good that you should sleep a bit so that you might enjoy the party even more. Wake up!"

Awakening at once and stretching contentedly, Mrs. Bjerke asked forgiveness for her unprecedented lapse of manners, but said she had enjoyed a most delightful sleep. When the hostess presented Olof Jonsson, the awakened sleeper laughed, understanding at once what had occurred.

"So I was the subject of a little experiment, eh?" she asked smiling. "Well, Engineer Jonsson, I do not mind. I have not felt so lively and rested for a long time!"

It could almost be stated arbitrarily that no hypnotist is conditioned to handle the various manifestations that may occur when a subject goes into mediumistic trance. In the first place, how will he recognize it unless he has had much experience with it before? Apparently the only way to identify the psychic from the ordinary citizen is by what he produces.

An old report from Wrentham, Massachusetts reveals how such things can get out of hand. Dated 1844, this very complete and detailed account was given by Emma Hardinge in

Modern American Spiritualism. She said she had it personally from Dr. Lyman B. Larkin, the physician in whose home
the incidents occurred. Since it is an old case and concerns
events of such a problematical nature, we cannot allow ourselves to offer it as evidence of anything. But it's an interesting story.

Mary Jane, the servant girl of Dr. Larkin had occasional
fits. This term was used long ago for onsets of epilepsy. It
also covered the weird kinds of trances that occasionally
occur to highly mediumistic persons whose talents are undis-
covered and untrained. When Mary Jane's spells began to
come on, Larkin learned to hypnotize her, ostensibly to relieve her problems—but he certainly made plenty for himself
in the process. Mrs. Hardinge says the girl did not respond to
Larkin's treatment too well at first; however, in time "clairvoyance of a most remarkable character supervened; she was
enabled during the mystic sleep to describe her own state and
that of a number of the doctor's patients of whom she had
never heard. When any difficult case was presented to Larkin, he had only, by a few passes, to place the girl into magnetic sleep," and then she would give a remarkable diagnosis
of the disease he wished to inquire about, and often, in addition, she would give a valuable and effective prescription.

She then began to say that she was seeing spirits who told
her how to cure the diseases she asked about. After that,
physical phenomena began to occur, the first being unex-
plained loud knockings in the room when Mary Jane was in
trance. They seemed to come from furniture sufficiently far
enough removed from her to preclude any suspicion that she
was herself doing it.

Under the influence of her good spirits, Mary Jane was
"skillful and sometimes philosophical and exalted; but occa-

sionally an influence seemed to possess her of the most profane and mischievous character." Mary Jane said he was a sailor boy, and it was apparently he who produced the psychokinetic phenomena. When he took her over she uttered the most blasphemous oaths and spoke the rudest speech. "At the same time," says Mrs. Hardinge, "the furniture was often moved about so violently by unseen hands, and heavy weights were lifted from place to place." Once, with the whole family at home, with the magnetized Mary Jane on a couch, and with every door in the house closed, a heavy flat iron last seen in the kitchen materialized in the presence of the family in the living room, and, furthermore, when Mrs. Larkin requested that the iron disappear, it vanished with equal suddenness and reappeared in the kitchen, again with every door remaining closed.

Many other spirits spoke through the girl, according to Mrs. Hardinge, and they revealed the most precise and accurate information about the names, places of birth and death, and other details regarding men and women she had never known. Larkin wrote down what was said and composed the history of 270 spirits "many of whose statements he took exceeding pains to prove, and in every instance found the description invariably correct in the minutest details."

Rumors of the shenanigans going on in the Larkin house went around the countryside, with the usual ugly exaggerations and innuendos. In the fall of 1847 a delegation of nine men, led by a minister, called on Larkin and demanded to know the truth. But they would not believe it when they heard it and insisted there had been scandalous behavior. Larkin offered to permit two or three members of the committee to live in his home, with board and room free, so they could observe the strange phenomena themselves and then report accordingly to the entire committee. They refused to do that, but would drop in from time to time and ply Mary Jane with countless questions.

At that time a Reverend Mr. Thatcher and his wife, orthodox and kindly people, moved into the Larkin home to observe the servant girl who behaved so strangely. After a week of thorough investigation, they left and prepared a circular that was sent to every minister within a twenty mile radius, absolving all concerned and hitherto suspected of fraud, deception, or connivance. They added that every clergyman should give these manifestations the "most serious and candid investigation." This did little good, for nobody paid attention. The Reverend Horace James of Wrentham, a particular enemy and slanderer of Larkin, was so convinced of his guilt that he persuaded three magistrates to organize a court, which in turn demanded that Larkin appear before it. Mary Jane was forcibly removed from the Larkin home and charged with "necromancy." She was convicted of that charge and also of sorcery and was sentenced to sixty days in solitary confinement in the Dedham jail.

Larkin was not legally charged with anything, but he was expelled from his church and told he could not return until he recanted and made a full confession of his crimes—as an accomplice to Mary Jane. Larkin insisted that he *did* believe in the communion of spirits and *did* realíze that they could and had communicated with him again and again through Mary Jane. But after stating this publicly for all to hear, he turned around and signed documents that declared that all he had said and maintained were the biggest lies ever spoken. He alibied this act by saying that his church meant so much to him that he perjured himself for it.

When Mrs. Hardinge interviewed him about the affair and

received the whole story from his lips, he told her he was ashamed of himself for signing the document denying the phenomena he had witnessed. Fat lot of good that did by then.

Mary Jane died a short time later. If any girl ever had an excuse for dying of a heart broken over the perfidy of her fellow men, she must be the one.

12. Role-Playing

JUST AS ONE may slip into various kinds of trance states when hypnotized, so he may also reach various levels of consciousness. Some rather amusing tests have been given to indicate this.

Edmund Gurney held the view that the main distinction of kind between the "alert" and the "deep" stage of hypnosis was to be found in the domain of memory, while memory also afforded the means for distinguishing the hypnotic state as a whole from the normal one. He invented a few procedures to test this, showing alternations of memory in the various stages of trance—the ideas impressed in the one stage being almost always forgotten in the other and then invariably remembered again when the former state recurred.

Gurney made trials with a considerable number of subjects in different parts of England and employed three hypnotizers, to each of whom the results were as new and surprising as they were at first to Gurney. Having several different hypnotists and numerous subjects indicated that the results were not because of any special idiosyncrasies of the individuals involved. The mode of effecting the passage from one stage to another usually consisted of gentle passes over the face, without bodily contact. Gurney wrote (*Proceedings SPR*, Vol. IV):

It is most impressive to find that a few noiseless movements of one person's fingers, at a short distance from another person's face, have completely obliterated that with which the latter's attention two or three seconds ago was entirely engrossed, and have brought back within his mental horizon that which no other means in the world—no other physical operation, not the clearest verbal reminder, not the fear of death, nor the offer of a one hundred pound reward—could have induced or enabled him to recall.

Gurney then reported a series of hypnotic memory experiments, using Mr. G. A. Smith as the hypnotist. There were several subjects who could reach three distinct stages of memory, which he called states A, B, and C. In each state the subject was told of some unusual incident, and his memory of that specific incident indicated which state he was in. One test follows:

In state A the subject was told that a foreign flag had been seen floating over the Pavilion. In state B he was told that two large dogs had been having a fight in Western Road. After discussing the topic of the A state, Smith made a few passes over the subject and then carried on the conversation without a pause:

Smith: People may well complain.
Subject: Yes.

Smith: Why?

Subject: Why, the nuisance—those dogs fighting in the Western Road. (This was the proper response for the B state, which he was in.)

Smith: I meant about the flag.

Subject: What flag? There are plenty of flags about. (The idea proper to the A stage is forgotten.)

Smith: No, I meant that cart running away in Montpelier Road. (This is a new idea, which henceforth belongs to the B class.

Subject: What cart? A cart running away! It's the horse that runs away. (He was then informed more particularly that a horse with a cart had bolted in Montpelier Road. Then deepening passes were continued.)

Smith: So they found it bottom upwards.

There was no answer; the subject had lapsed into sleep. He was called by name, and a few reverse passes were made. Then he awoke with an "Eh?" He had been brought into stage C. Smith told him that a very high tide had washed a boat on the beach, but that after a time it had drifted ashore. The subject was on the verge of lapsing into unconsciousness, and he did lapse immediately after being told this. He was roused, and Smith said: "That's the effect of not tying it securely."

The subject's answer now showed that the rousing had carried him over stage C and that he was once more in stage B.

Subject: Tied? They never tie them.

Smith: No wonder it was washed away then.

Subject: Washed away? Did it go over the cliff?

Smith: No, what do you mean?

Subject: That horse and cart you were talking about.

Some reverse passes were now made to bring the subject into the A state.

Smith: I dare say it will get knocked about on the beach.

Subject: What knocked about?

Smith: What I was telling you about.

Subject: Why, have they taken it on the beach now?

Smith: What do you mean?

Subject: That large flag.

The subject was now carried down without pause into the state of deep sleep—the most certain way of lighting on stage C being to go beyond it in this way and then to revive the subject just enough to enable him to understand and answer. He was called by name several times, and a few reverse passes were made before he answered: "Eh? What?"

Smith now replied in words that would apply equally to carts or boats; but the subject understood them to apply to boats—the C idea.

Smith: Is it customary to tie them?

Subject: Yes.

Smith: I thought you said it wasn't. (The subject had said before that it was not customary to tie *carts*.)

Subject: Oh, yes. Sometimes they tie them to capstans, sometimes to larger vessels. (Some upward passes were made, and then Smith said: "Did you say they tie them to a capstan?")

Subject: No, they throw the reins loose over the horse's back.

Smith: A lot of people saw it coming down.

Subject: What, the horse and cart?

Here is the reappearance of stage B; and proceeding again on the upward or lightening course, they found the A idea—the flag on the Pavilion—duly remembered. This testing occurred on February 28. On March 2 the same process was briefly repeated, and it was learned that the subject still remembered each of the topics already mentioned when its appropriate stage was reached, and at that stage alone.

Another of these games of Cross Questions and Crazy Answers was undertaken by Mrs. Henry Sidgwick, the wife of the first president of the Society for Psychical Research and an ardent but objective researcher in her own rights. In her experience, one man was found who could maintain eight distinct trains of memory—each recurring when the corresponding depth of trance was reached.

In these various stages of trance we invariably find the subject saying what is expected of him. In addition, as Samuel Glasner stated in "Social Psychological Aspects of Hypnosis": "It is incontrovertible . . . that hypnotized subjects do demonstrate a remarkably heightened capacity for acting out various roles which are suggested to them." It should be realized that good subjects possess a remarkable ability to fantasize under hypnosis. Such fantasies seem very real and vivid, and the subject is not aware that they are fantasies.

Dr. John Björkhem of Stockholm, a physician so modern in his thinking that he spends a great deal of time in parapsychological experimentation, undertook extensive research in this area and made thousands of tests with various subjects. As a psychiatrist, he used both mental patients and normal people. On repetition, he found confirmation of early reports and had astounding results with a few of his subjects. The ability to fantasize was evident in the great majority of his tests. The subject would report what he thought he saw when traveling to some distant scene, but it was not always what actually was occurring there. Yet again, in some cases the reports were correct in detail, revealing that an instance of traveling clairvoyance had been stumbled upon.

This is why it is difficult to be sure just what is going on when subjects are age regressed. They will play the role of the age to which they are told to return, and it may or may not be exact fact. Still, there are interesting incidents that reveal that actual regression does frequently occur. Boris Sidis, one of the pioneers of psychopathology, recounted in *The Psychology of Suggestion* how he hypnotized a subject, suggested to him that he was only ten years old, and asked him to write something. What was written was his signature —not in English but in script used by Eastern Jews, going from right to left across the page. The subject's brother, who witnessed the experiment, explained that the subject had known no other alphabet when he was ten years old and that there was an actual resemblance to the handwriting he had exhibited as a child. Sidis' subject had not lost his capacity to understand English, however, since the commands and suggestions were given in that language.

Age regression has come to be an excellent therapeutic tool in psychoanalysis. If an individual is regressed to the age of seven, say, and relives a previously suppressed traumatic experience that has been affecting his life ever since, talking of it and recognizing it can usually relieve the patient of his symptoms. Hypnotic age regression in some areas is making slow but steady progress, but in psychotherapy it has taken giant strides. From all parts of the United States and from all parts of the world, clinical use of hypnotic age regression is being reported in scientific papers.

"Just as in most areas of hypnosis," says Sidney A.

Schneider, a certified hypnotherapist, in "Report on Hypnotic Age Regression" in *Fate*, October 1965, "there is no agreement on the nature of regression. Since its discovery in 1887 it has been the subject of constant controversy." The main basis for the debate over hypnotic age regression stems from the human factor; that is, that differences in personality and investigative experience among hypnotists influence their theories.

"They look at age regression subjectively as well as objectively," says Schneider, "and each sees it in a different light. The various differences, however, now have settled into two theories: Hypnotic age regression is either a valid phenomenon or it is role-playing—acting out a part that the subject believes is expected of him."

A polygraph (lie detector) test given by Dr. Milton Kline of Long Island University resulted in the conclusion: "The subject's involvement in this experience is quite real to him, and therefore is not experienced as deception."

So all hypnotists should take into consideration the fact that an entranced subject wants to please the hypnotist and often carries out what he thinks is expected of him. Sometimes he is aware that he is doing this, sometimes not. And here is a very good point brought out long ago by the nineteenth-century French researcher Dr. H. Bernheim: "When a physician employs hypnosis with a patient, it is wise always to be aware of who may be hypnotizing whom."

Interesting evidence of how the hypnotee tries to cooperate is given by Dr. A. M. Ludwig (*Newsletter* of the Parapsychology Foundation, July–August 1967), speaking of the work started at the Federal Narcotics Center in Lexington, Kentucky. Referring to his own interest in trying to learn a little more about the effect of narcotic drugs and to evaluate this effect on addicts, Ludwig pointed out that there are two states that must be studied in the drug addict. There is, first, the state in which the addict takes the drug and has a variety of experiences: emotional, subjective, psychological, physiological. Then there is the withdrawal state, when the drug is abruptly withdrawn, and there are revealed a variety of physiological, emotional, and psychological changes. He then went on to describe an experiment conducted with a colleague, in which they attempted "to understand the effect the psyche had on the drug effects as well as the withdrawal effects." They selected eleven subjects who had all experienced such withdrawal symptoms, who were post-drug addicts and patients at the hospital, and they trained them in hypnosis in order to give them by suggestion the feeling they were back on the streets of their old home town (which was New York City for most of them). While in the trance, they were encouraged to believe they were giving themselves a shot of heroin. Dr. Ludwig says: "We trained them by suggestion. These were well-trained hypnotic subjects, with something like five hours of preparation beforehand. They were able to imagine these effects not only with great vividness, but they were also able to show the physiological effects."

During the experiment blood pressure readings were made; pulse rate, pupillary size, respiration were recorded. The behavior of the subjects was carefully noted. The better ones removed their belts, wrapped them around their arms, pulling them tight, and gave themselves shots with imaginary needles. It all communicated a typical picture of addicts taking heroin. They sat back in their chairs, sighed, and soon drifted off into the familiar narcotic high, with the lower lip drooping and with simultaneous drooling.

Then, when the subjects were told—still in trance, it must be emphasized—that they had just been picked up by the police and placed in jail with their heroin supply cut off twenty-four hours earlier, they began showing authentic withdrawal symptoms: yawning, eyes tearing, noses running, with some of the men groaning because of aches in their legs.

Ludwig noted that he and Dr. J. Levine had conducted many experiments jointly, adding:

One of the conclusions that we did come to with our work with narcotic drugs and evoking these symptoms—withdrawal effects as well as drug effects—was that even though we were able to produce very realistic drug effect states and very realistic withdrawal effect stages which were significantly different from control conditions (and we had faking subjects and acting subjects as a comparison here), we did definitely feel that it was an "as if" state, that is, it approached the real state, but wasn't quite the real state. In other words, the subjects themselves, as we questioned them afterwards, said they *almost* felt as though they had this experience, but it wasn't quite the real thing. . . . Now, Dr. Levine and I also did this on a couple of occasions with a subject who had an LSD experience, and we tried to evoke it again. It turned out most unsatisfactory. He really worked at trying to re-experience this, but it wasn't the genuine experience. My guess is that you can come close—"almost" and "as if," but not really undergo the real experience.

An interesting postscript was reported by Dr. Levine, which concerned a subject in a hypnodelic state who reported that he felt uncomfortable because of the vague assurance that he was being watched by two people who were trying to read his mind. In fact, and completely unknown to him in his normal state, Dr. Levine and Dr. Ludwig were observing him behind a one-way mirror in a connecting room.

A really classic, if gruesome, story that indicates how a hypnotized person can produce material that is relevant comes from the introductory and biographical note affixed to the Catalogue Raisonné du Musée Wiertz (1865) by Dr. S. Watteau. Here is found a detailed description of an extremely curious hypnotic experiment in which Antonie Joseph Wiertz, a celebrated painter, was the subject, and a friend, a prison doctor in Brussels, the hypnotist.

Wiertz had long been haunted by a desire to know whether thought persisted in a head severed from its trunk. Since the doctor had more than once put Wiertz into trance and since a murder trial had been causing a great sensation in Belgium, the painter evolved a really spooky idea. When the trial ended in the condemnation of the accused, the prison doctor was able to arrange to carry it out. He obtained permission for the hypnotized Wiertz and a friend, Dr. D——, to hide under the guillotine, close to where the head of the condemned would roll into a basket.

Preparations for this were made by the doctor by putting the painter through a regular course of hypnotic suggestion, and when he was in the sleep state commanding him to identify himself with various people and read their thoughts and penetrate into their psychical and mental states. On the day of execution, ten minutes before the arrival of the condemned man, Wiertz, the doctor, and two witnesses crawled underneath the guillotine, where they were entirely hidden from sight. The painter was then put into trance and told to identify himself with the criminal. He was to follow his thoughts and feelings and express them aloud. He was also suggested to take special note of mental conditions during decapitation, so that when the head fell into the basket he could penetrate the brain and give an account of its last thoughts. Wiertz became entranced almost immediately, and the four friends soon understood by the sounds overhead that the executioner was conducting the condemned to the scaffold, and in another minute the guillotine would do its work. The hypnotized Wiertz manifested extreme distress and begged to be demagnetized, as his sense of oppression was insupportable. It was too late, however—the knife fell!

"What do you feel? What do you see?" asked the doctor. Wiertz writhed convulsively and replied, "Lightning! a thunderbolt falls! It thinks; it sees!"

"What thinks and sees?"

"The head. It suffers horribly. It thinks and feels but does not understand what has happened. It seeks its body and feels that the body must join it. It still waits for the supreme blow for death, but death does not come." As Wiertz spoke, the head fell into the basket and lay looking at them horribly; its arteries still palpitating. It was only after some moments of suffering that the guillotined head apparently at least became aware that it was separated from its body. Wiertz became calmer and seemed exhausted, while the doctor resumed his questions.

The painter then gave a long mental scanning of the situation:

I fly through space like a top spinning through fire. But am I dead? Is it all over? If only they could let me join my body again! Have pity! Give it back to me and let me live again. I remember all. There are the judges in red robes. I hear the sentence. Oh! my wretched wife and children. I am abandoned. If only you would put my body to me, I should be with you once more. You refuse? All the same, I love you, my poor babies. Miserable wretch that I am I have covered you with blood. When will this finish? Or is not a murderer condemned to eternal punishment?

As Wiertz spoke these words the witnesses thought they saw the eyes of the decapitated head open wide with a look of unmistakable suffering and beseeching. The painter continued his lamentations: "No, such suffering cannot endure forever; God is merciful. All that belongs to earth is fading away. I see in the distance a little light glittering like a diamond. I feel a calm stealing over me. What a good sleep I shall have! What joy!"

These were the last words the painter spoke. He was still entranced, but no longer replied to the questions put by the doctor. They then approached the head, and Dr. D—— touched the forehead, the temples, and the teeth. They were cold. The head was dead.

In the Wiertz Gallery in Brussels soon after that were to be found three pictures of a guillotined head, presumably the outcome of this appalling experience.

13. Age Regression

THE BEST ILLUSTRATION of possible role-playing when one is hypnotized is age regression purportedly to past lives. Sometimes this is used to support the theory of reincarnation (the doctrine of successive lives spent by each soul on this earth). As we have already seen, one of the things known for sure about hypnosis is that some entranced subjects will make every attempt to please the hypnotist, and often they carry out what is expected of them. The hypnotist's own beliefs about what he is doing, the tone of his voice, his manner, and his mode of procedure cause the subject to enact faithfully the role thereby handed to him. This is then taken by the hypnotist as evidence confirming the correctness of his original belief. So if he tells a subject to regress to a life previous to the one he is now living, and believes that this is possible, something that purports to be an account of a past life is usually produced. Because this is true, age regression is complicated, and past life regression is problematical, to say the least. Yet occasionally a case occurs that gives us pause and makes us wonder.

The case of Mlle. Hélène Smith was reported in the early 1900s by European psychologist Professor T. Flournoy in a book called *From India to the Planet Mars*. A best seller of that day, the book tells of the regressions to various past lives of a Swiss girl whom he gives the pseudonym Hélène Smith. The young woman was not and never had been a paid medium, but she gave séances for her friends simply because she enjoyed them. As Flournoy's book was being written, Hélène occupied a leading post on the staff of a large Geneva store.

When hypnotized and age regressed, she had many fantastic stories to tell about her alleged past lives, most of which perhaps suffered from the general fault of aiming too high. Marie Antoinette and an Indian princess named Simandini, wife of a minor rajah, were two of her incarnations, and she also reported a lifetime on Mars!

Interestingly enough, when Flournoy tried to verify her accounts to see if there was anything factual in them, although many anachronisms occurred, he occasionally found bits and pieces of information that seemed quite accurate. In researching her Indian princess, for instance, he was unable to find any references to such persons for some time; but he finally did locate an account in a very obscure history book that checked with her statements. He doubted that she could have had access to a copy of this book. Most puzzling was that Hélène, in trance and regressed to the Oriental life, seemed to have a good knowledge of Sanskrit. Yet her specimen of handwriting that purported to be Marie Antoinette's was nothing like that of the real queen.

When she reported on her life on Mars she drew pictures of Martian people and landscapes and both spoke and wrote what she said was the Martian language, using a vocabulary of five hundred words. However, in analyzing the language, Flournoy found that it was a childish, although elaborate, imitation of French—her native tongue.

A study that revealed results more questionable than Flournoy's was published in 1911 in Paris by Colonel Albert de Rochas. Titled *Les Vies Successives*, it described experiments with some nineteen persons in what was called magnetic sleep. De Rochas apparently regressed his subjects to various ages down to the time of their birth, then into intrauterine life, then purportedly to existence as discarnate spirits, and then, still farther back, to one or more earlier lives. Age regressions were induced by means of longitudinal passes, and age progressions, which he also attempted, by means of transverse passes. However, an incident in one of his experiments led de Rochas to remark: "Apparently the mode of magnetization, that is, the direction of the passes, has no great importance." He did, however, hold to the idea of a magnetic fluid and of the efficacy upon it of the passes.

In 1904 de Rochas had regressed an eighteen-year-old girl, Josephine, to the time of her birth; then he continued to make longitudinal passes. This brought forward purported consciousness of the intrauterine period and then of a discarnate period preceding conception. Further deepening of the trance then resulted in the manifestation of a personality whose nature at first puzzled the hypnotist, for it would not say who nor where it was. He eventually replied in gruff tones, with a man's voice, that he was Jean-Claude Bourdon, born in 1812 in the village of Champvent, district of Polliat, where he died at seventy. He gave various details of his life, but subsequent inquiry turned up no evidence that such a man had lived at that time and place.

Deepening Josephine's trance brought out the personality of a wicked old woman, who called herself Philomene Charpigny. She said that she was born in 1702, that she had married a man named Carteron in 1732 at Chevroux, and that her grandfather, Pierre Machon, had lived at Oxan. De Rochas states in a footnote that families by the names of Charpigny and Carteron did exist at Oxan and Chevroux, but that he found no positive trace of Philomene herself. Additional deepening of the trance brought out that, in previous lives, Josephine had been a girl who had died in infancy and before that a bandit who robbed and killed.

Then came the shamefaced avowal that, in a life anterior to the bandit incarnation, she had been a big ape!

Age progression into the future is another chancy technique, unless you are sure your subject is highly clairvoyant and is able to produce precognition as a medium might. But it is also attempted on a hit or miss basis by many hypnotists. Leslie LeCron, a psychologist who has specialized in hypnosis, says in "Hypnosis in the Production of Psi Phenomena":

The question then arises as to whether events described are actually precognition of future happenings or merely fantasies. Unquestionably most subjects will produce only fantasies and will describe something which will not actually take place. In 1952 when Truman was a candidate for the presidency, this writer age progressed a subject to the day following the election, it then being a few days prior to election day. The subject was told to see the headlines of the morning newspaper and state who had won. He reported the headline to be TRUMAN ASSASSINATED. It is not too difficult to guess as to the political views of this subject!

De Rochas attempted to progress Josephine to later ages in her present life and brought out various episodes that did not come to pass. When she was carried farther ahead, to give incidents in future lives, she said she would die at the age of seventy, then reincarnate first as a girl, Elise, who would die when three years old. She would next be Marie, daughter of a man by the name of Edmond Baudin, who would run a shoe store at Saint-Germain-du-Mont-d'Or and whose wife's name would be Rosalie.

De Rochas stated that "these revelations, when it has been possible to test their veridicality, have not in general corresponded to the facts." In some cases numerous anachronisms occurred. And in some cases, where details susceptible to verification were mentioned, the attempt subsequently made to corroborate them failed to do so. Thus, de Rochas was on the whole far from fully convinced that the regressions under hypnosis that he related really were regressions to earlier lives of the persons described. A big ape! Now really.

The late C. J. Ducasse, formerly Professor Emeritus of Philosophy at Brown University and a leading international figure in his field, evaluated the de Rochas cases in *The Belief in a Life After Death*:

In the absence of definite verification of the details they relate, the most plausible explanation of the facts appears to be that they are effects of suggestion and/or of stimulation of the mythopoeic imagination in the trance state. One feature of de Rochas' cases, which also points to this explanation, is that in almost all of them the purported earlier lives of those French subjects are likewise lives as French men or women; which, of course, especially for persons of simple minds, and who had never read much or travelled abroad, would be the psychologically easiest and most natural kinds of earlier lives to imagine.

Ducasse himself had a case of age regression much more interesting than any of de Rochas'. In February 1906, in

New York City, he was present at two experiments in which the subject was a young woman whose name he had forgotten; and a physician named Dr. Morris Stark was the hypnotist. Ducasse recorded in shorthand at the time the whole of both incidents. The girl was familiar with the idea of reincarnation and understood that the experiment was to be an attempt to regress her consciousness to a time before her birth. She had been previously regressed by the same doctor, at which time the name Zoe had been obtained as one of her earlier appellations.

In Ducasse's record there were hardly any items that would lend themselves to verification. "Hence," he says, "such correspondence as may obtain between the statements of the entranced subject and historical fact is hardly evidence of reincarnation or even of paranormal cognition."

When first regressed, the girl was asked to tell where she was, and she said: "It is very warm." She described walking under a blue unclouded sky by blue water on which there were ships. She did not know her name, but the beautiful trees and plants, the city in the distance, and the people around her enchanted her.

"How are the people dressed?" she was asked.

"They wear loose, beautiful gowns, not like others I have seen. Their arms are bare; they are talking."

"What language?"

"Who are you?" she countered.

"I am a friend of yours."

She then spoke of the city on hills and said she lived over there by the water, but she did not know the name of it. Young men were playing games, because it was some feast day. People had flowers in their hair. She was about twenty-nine; she had slaves who carried her in a litter. Her people had many gods. Their money was sesterces. A poet named Marcus read to her. Her husband's name, she eventually remembered, was Flavius.

In response to many questions, which as a rule tried not to lead her, she revealed much knowledge of ancient Rome. Then, right in the midst of her conversation she said: "I will go to sleep; you will not mind if I go to sleep? I am so tired. I don't know why. There are clouds; where are you? . . . You have taken me somewhere else. You are taking me across the water. We are going south." And then she was someone else named Ula Desthenes. She seemed to be a temple virgin in Egypt and gave considerable data about the temple ceremonies, the buildings, and the conditions of the times. When asked how she was dressed she said: "I have a white robe, very rich." There were jewels on her arms. She wore anklets and sometimes she walked barefoot.

On February 25, 1906, the doctor, right after hypnotizing the girl, called: "Zoe, Zoe, how do you do? Good morning, how are you?" And Zoe replied. Professor Ducasse says: "The difference between the tone and the manner of the Zoe personality and those of either the Roman or Egyptian personality was most impressive."

Zoe then proceeded to say: "I can't see. Who called me by that name. It is long since anyone called me that; it was Zoe. Where do you come from? You speak a dead tongue . . . something . . . it is confused. Those were happy days in the streets."·

The doctor asked: "What country is this?"

She answered: "A warm country. Zoe, it is good to hear the name again. The wife of Dedro."

"How old are you now?"

"That I forget. I am too old to be alive. Everything is

gone, nothing remains but sorrow and hunger; I have had a hard life." She was in a big city with snow-capped mountains off in the distance. Camels were used to carry things. There are also little shaggy horses. "They don't look like any horses," she added.

Naturally one wonders why, if she were living a role in a past life, she would know the animals did not look like horses. Or even know the word for horses, or what they were. The terminology used was always modern even when discussing ancient times. It is all very confusing, really.

I once saw two lightly entranced young girls age regressed and asked to tell what went on before they came into this life on earth. The one who believed in reincarnation immediately produced some medieval history that she claimed to be living in colorful fashion. The other, who had no conviction about rebirth, became a water fairy or sprite. No matter how she was led to explain it, or to grow into something more useful to the hypnotist, she could only answer that she was swimming in or flitting about over a rocky pool. She was finally given up as a bad job.

In 1943, Ducasse had a "life reading" done by Edgar Cayce, who had added such material to his repertoire by then. According to it, in Ducasse's preceding incarnation his name had been Jean de Larquen, and he had come to America from France as an intelligence officer associated with Lafayette. Ducasse, who was himself from France, made numerous inquiries in an attempt to discover if anyone either in the United States or his homeland in revolutionary times had ever borne that name. He found no records of such a character.

Cayce had been giving his medical readings and helping a great many people with them when a well-to-do printer,

Arthur Lammers, approached him with the problem of human destiny. Cayce, in trance, gave Lammers' horoscope and then added cryptically: "He was once a monk." Lammers and others then attempted to elicit from Cayce "life readings" instead of the usual "health readings," which had so much clinical value to so many. So then when the sleeping Cayce was supplied with the name of a person and the date and place of his birth, he gave details about past incarnations. Cayce alleged about himself, when he was asleep, that he had been a physician in an earlier life. This was supposed to account for his ability to give medical advice. Oddly enough, however, his prescriptions were frequently homeopathic, and he was an enthusiast about osteopaths wherever he felt they could be helpful.

About Cayce's life readings Professor Ducasse said:

These purported to report one or more earlier lives on earth of the person concerned, the name he or she had borne then, and the actions or experiences in those past lives which had as remote consequences in the present life certain features of body, mind, or character, and certain special abilities. Although in these readings the persons concerned were generally entire strangers to Cayce and far away at the time, his delineations of their present personality and vocational capacities was often surprisingly accurate.

Dr. Gina Cerminara, a psychologist who made a study of the records of these Cayce readings, stated in *Many Mansions* that obscure historical details mentioned in the accounts of earlier lives of some of the persons who had life readings—including "the names of obscure former personalities . . . in the locality"—have been verified by historical records.

Ducasse says of this:

But in the absence of citation of specific cases where details of an earlier life were given . . . and where careful verification of those details was made and is on record, the mere statement that such verification has been made does not constitute for us empirical evidence that the Cayce life readings really describe past incarnations of the persons concerned. And, although correct delineation of the present character and abilities of strangers at a distance would require clairvoyance of a high order, such delineation in itself has no relevance to the matter of rebirth.

Under these circumstances, the chief importance of the Cayce life readings in connection with the question as to the reality of reincarnation is the suggestion it affords that the hypnotic trance may be a means of bringing back in certain persons memories of presently verifiable details of earlier lives of their own; and possibly a means of arousing in exceptional individuals retrocognition of the lives of deceased persons, such as Cayce's life readings purportedly constituted, but with presently verifiable details.

Loring G. Williams in a *Fate* article entitled "Reincarnation of a Civil War Victim" offers a case that seems to bring fairly secure evidence of some sort of supernormal knowledge. Whether it was reincarnation or retrocognition (supernormal knowledge of the past) or even spirit influence, it is impossible to ascertain.

Williams, a high school teacher in Vermont, dabbled in hypnosis, particularly age regression, for many years. He points out that in practically all cases people who can be regressed to their childhood can also be regressed beyond, sometimes hundreds of years into the past, to describe what appear to be previous lives. But however fascinating it is to hear and record these stories of past lives, it is of little scientific value unless the story can be proved.

While holding weekly sessions in his home, during which

volunteers were regressed, Williams continually looked for a hypnotic subject with a story that could be checked. But he found that many subjects when regressed are hazy about details. They cannot remember their full names in their alleged past lives, or their parents' names. They're not sure where they live, are unable to give other details needed for checking a story. Others who may give vivid details usually describe an existence so long ago, or in such a remote place, that verification is out of the question. "And so," he says, "I heard many interesting stories but none that could be checked. Then along came George Field, a fifteen-year-old neighbor of mine."

With no particular interest in history or geography and no past experience in North Carolina, George produced the case history of a man of Jefferson, North Carolina who lived from 1832 to 1863. This was recent enough and close enough geographically for checking. Consequently during the next summer vacation the teacher and his pupil set out for the site of the action. They did not discover historical records of the actual person allegedly produced by the regression—Jonathan Powell—nor of any of his close relatives except a Mary Powell who had once bought property there. She had been stated by Jonathan to be his grandmother.

Prior to the trip, all the data Jonathan had given about his life had been recorded for the sake of checking the evidence. When the teacher and his pupil reached Ashe County, which George, as Jonathan, had previously named correctly, the boy was hypnotized, and Jonathan was allowed to look over his home country. He hardly recognized it because it had changed so much, and the macadam on the highways bothered tremendously one who had only known dirt roads; yet the big mountain back of the town was apparently the "good sized hill over there" he had mentioned. There was a river called South Fork, and there was a nearby town named Clifton, as the records reveal he had stated. Also on the tape Jonathan named a minister, a Mr. Brown. Williams found there had been a Mr. Brown who was a circuit-riding preacher in the area at the time Jonathan claimed to have known him. He mentioned Carter's store and Mrs. Abby. There was now no record of the store, but there were Carters in the area in Jonathan's time and also an Abby family.

Williams writes:

Perhaps the most significant part of the tape is the description of Jonathan's death. He claimed to have been shot by Yankee soldiers in 1863 because he would not sell them potatoes for ten cents a bushel. He stated these soldiers were wearing gray uniforms but that they were not southerners. I felt he had to be wrong about this. As far as any Civil War records I could find were concerned there were no Yankee troops in North Carolina in 1863, and everyone knows the Yankees did not wear gray. Nevertheless, Jonathan was right. The local historian told me that at that time, there were bands of renegades who came down from the north, usually from Kentucky, using the war as an excuse to raid and plunder. They could well have been dressed in gray because they would have stolen their uniforms.

All this has convinced Williams that he has proved reincarnation. Another observer might think it more likely to indicate retrocognition. And then, because the hypnotic trance is so similar to the mediumistic trance, could there not be the possibility that when George was hypnotized he became a medium as some of our clairvoyants of the past have done? Perhaps he was being influenced by the spirit of Jonathan Powell, who had lived in Jefferson, North Carolina, and was still attempting to make his presence known when an occasion occurred that someone in a trance state was receptive to his thoughts.

There are many ways to interpret age regression evidence, and, for that matter, the idea of reincarnation itself. A recent, delightful Gothic-like novel by Florence Stevenson titled *A Feast of Eggshells* gives an amusing angle on the subject. When the baby Pamela Gabrielle is born, and the doctor spanks her, she utters a naughty four-letter word, almost giving nervous breakdowns to the doctors and nurses in attendance. From then on, it is evident that the spirit of an earthy woman has been captured by (or has reincarnated into, as the author of the book prefers to call it) the body of the beautiful little girl. She is typical of the many historical types who give birth to a child and then die and want to come back so they can keep an eye on their babies. This mother is finally released with all her profane vitality when a psychiatrist hypnotises the child. From then on she talks constantly in her vulgar fashion, demanding to be taken to her "kid," as she calls her baby Dottie. Descriptions of the angelic looking five-year-old with the mind of a gangster's moll and her efforts to see her kid are hilarious. So also is the presentation of how the world goes wild when it is learned that she is the first genuine proof of life after death since Christ. The crowds and the publicity are overwhelming to all concerned. The tiny tyke who is so avidly seeking to be rejoined with her baby is even named Mother of the Year!

With these subjects as complicated as they are, a hypnotist who wanted to be mean could get a girl all mixed up. Eric Cuddon admits it in *Hypnosis: Its Meaning and Practice*, telling how he suggested to Miss A—— in the somnambulic state that in a previous incarnation she had been a slave girl purchased by Nero. The subject claimed to remember the incident quite clearly and stated that the Emperor had fallen for her long and lovely hair. (She had often said, in her waking moments, that she had long, lovely hair when she was a girl.)

About a week later she was asked by one of her friends in the course of conversation whether she believed in the possibility of reincarnation. Her reply was an emphatic affirmative; she was quite certain that in a previous life she had been the favorite slave of the *Egyptian* Emperor Nero!

The subconscious can even take information previously known by the subject but not recalled and turn it into a dramatization. A good illustration of this was given in the Toronto *Star Weekly*, June 9, 1956, quoting Dr. Harold Rosen. A patient regressed ostensibly to a past life began to speak in Oscan, a language not in use since the third century B.C. He was asked to write it out and he did, carefully printing each word. The doctor said: "This made identification possible. He was reciting in Oscan one of a series of magical curses which usually were inscribed on lead plates thin enough to be rolled up and thrown in graves, so the thrower could gain control over various of the infernal deities. Our patient had never studied Latin, had never heard of Oscan, and on nonhypnotic levels was completely unaware of what he had said or written." Subsequent inquiries elicited the information that once on a previous occasion the subject had glanced at a book lying open in the library on which were the words "The Curse of Vibia." Under it the curse was printed in the Oscan language, and somehow it had imprinted itself in his unconscious.

14. Multiple Personality

ONE OF THE MOST curious manifestations to be studied by the psychologist is the occasional instance of what is known as multiple, or split, personality. It occurs rarely, but when it does, the only apparent treatment for it is hypnosis.

The best known modern account of this is in *The Three Faces of Eve* by Drs. C. H. Thigpen and H. M. Cleckley, about a fascinating patient of theirs. The names given the protagonist are, of course, fictitious. The story in brief will illustrate how what appear to be completely differing submerged personalities of the same person seem to take control of the body on various occasions.

When Eve White arrived at the doctors' office for psychiatric treatment, she was a meek, overcontrolled housewife with some religious and matrimonial conflicts. Her symptoms included headaches and possible blackouts. Hypnosis was used in therapy. About a year later Eve went holidaying with a relative and seemed to be an entirely different person while she was away. She had a jolly time and disowned her husband when he came to take her home. When her old self spontaneously returned, it was apparently amnesic about the holiday period. The next exploit of the alternating personality was to buy lots of expensive clothes of a more flamboyant type than Eve White would have considered. White, of course, did not know what was happening. She would just go to sleep, and when she woke it was some long time later, and there was the clothing she had bought while asleep.

At one time Eve expressed anxiety about hearing voices. This is the only indication of anything of a psychic nature in this case, and it could have been pathological instead. Anyway, little attention was paid to the possibility of supernormal aspects of the case by these modern doctors who know nothing about what they probably consider such "mystical and magical notions" and care less.

One day, while visiting the doctors, Eve Black made her first appearance to them. Her personality, not troubled by neurasthenic symptoms, was happy, irresponsible, sexually attractive, and provocative—out for a good time. She was always definitely nettled by White's careful conscientiousness, as White was equally upset by her lack of it.

After that, whichever personality came out under hypnosis underwent analysis with the doctors; matrimonial problems were discussed with both and finally resolved in divorce. Then a third personality, called Jane, appeared. She was amnesic for both other phases, quieter and more dignified than Black, better adjusted than White. It was discovered that a traumatic experience when Jane was five had resulted in the split, and the three personalities were finally resolved into a healthier and more mature Jane. All these personalities eventually became a more mature synthesis called Eve Lancaster.

Psychiatrist Dr. Nandor Fodor, in his review of this book for *Tomorrow*, spoke of the heroic work Thigpen and Cleckley did to help this patient: "They battled against the unknown, facing their task with courage and scientific humility. Without the wise and sympathetic treatment accorded to all three personalities, they could not have won their cooperation and Eve White would have ended her life in a mental institution."

Fodor concluded: "The book is written in novelistic style, making literature out of psycho-pathology. No psychiatric education is needed for its full enjoyment. No one should miss it." It was also made into a movie that won an Oscar for its star Joanne Woodward and showed by its popularity that everyone loves such a mystery.

But what is it that really happens when a personality splits? We have to do a lot of thinking about it in an effort to understand it, and even then it will not be completely clear. Edgar Wirt in "Dualism is With Us Again" says:

Before modern times there was little question about the dual nature of man as *body* and *soul*. One of the modern revolts was to question and discredit the separateness of the soul, or the reality of soul as a separate aspect of man. This was one phase of the modern assault on dualism. There still remained, however, the practical differences in physical, mental, emotional, and social development. More and more we have put all these under the one tent of comprehensive education—education of the "whole man." And the whole man tends to become basically a physical organism of wondrous complexity, by which all his other functions and capacities were to be accountable.

Then came another split: conscious and subconscious, or the unconscious in man. . . . It was easy enough to say that there were only different aspects of one individual mind or consciousness.

That is what psychiatrists who deal with split personalities try to do—to see the individual mind as a whole with, you might say, various phases. The idea of the possibility that the old-fashioned concepts of possession or obsession by an external entity could be involved is under no circumstances considered, because that is not the modern way of thinking. And, indeed, there is not much evidence of such a likelihood in the Eve case. Fodor speaks of that: "It is an open question, however, whether the involvement of a spiritualistically oriented investigator might not have given [that kind of] coloring to Eve Black or Jane." Fodor thinks Black would have been suited ideally for the role of an obsessing entity and "there can be little doubt that she would have eagerly seized on the suggestion had it been put forward." Which does not mean that it would have been the truth. Even one disposed to look for supernormal involvement has to admit that it is not always evident.

Such cases undoubtedly were thought of as possession in the past, however, and so it was not until the advent of psychotherapy in the latter part of the last century that the idea of multiple personality occurred to the doctors who became involved with anything of that nature. And then it became a fad for a time. Many cases of hysteria were erroneously diagnosed as split personality.

J. P. Sutcliffe and Jean Jones of the University of Sydney, Australia, in "Personal Identity, Multiple Personality, and Hypnosis," wrote:

Acceptance of hypnotic behaviors as transformations of the subject by the hypnotist facilitated acceptance of the idea of people spontaneously "transforming" themselves. . . . Psychology was struggling for a foothold as an empirical science when the notion of multiple personality was being elaborated. Empirical procedures were marked by a lack of controls; selection of anecdotal evidence was the main means of data gathering, particularly in abnormal psychology. Findings were widely generalized and woven into a fabric of sweeping theorizing. Theories were often very crude and were readily modified on the basis of slim evidence.

Thus a few of the old and interesting cases might better be classified as "Disintegrations of Personality," as Myers listed them, rather than as multiple personalities. They are curious enough to mention briefly here, however, because they almost invariably showed some kind of supernormal manifestations.

The case of Mollie Fancher was originally described by Judge Abram H. Dailey as a rather disconnected narrative containing abstracts of a diary kept by Miss Fancher's aunt, a series of signed statements made by friends, and a number of reprints of articles that had originally appeared in the daily papers. It was published under the title: "Mollie Fancher: the Brooklyn Enigma." *An Authentic Statement of Facts in the Life of Mary J. Fancher, the Psychological Marvel of the Nineteenth Century.*

Miss Fancher was born August 16, 1848. When she was sixteen she was thrown from a horse and severely injured, and later the lower part of her body suddenly was paralyzed. After other accidents she became seriously ill, had convulsions, and soon lost in rapid succession sight, speech, and hearing. Her history was that of a hysteric of the worst type. But even when she was blindest she seemed to possess supernormal powers of vision. It is claimed that she repeatedly read sealed letters, described events at a distance, and found lost articles.

The case of Anna Winsor, a woman with an extreme form of hysteroepilepsy, with very violent and frequent convulsions and intervals of insane delusions, was recorded in detail for over two-and-a-half years—1860 to 1863—by a Dr. Barrows. Her trouble started with what appeared to be typhoid fever. Then suddenly while she was convalescing, without any apparent cause she had a relapse of fever, raving delirium in which she pulled out much of her hair, convulsions, and loss of consciousness. She was hypnotized, but no cure was ever effected.

Among Barrows' notes about Anna Winsor:

April 9th—became deaf; great pain in head; is conscious of her suffering most of the time. Commences bead work; makes three bead baskets; does it all with her left hand [she was not naturally left handed but had taken a dislike to her right arm and hand and refused to use them]; threads her needle, strings her beads, makes her baskets; works alike by daylight, gaslight, twilight, and in the dark. I have sat by her in the evening and witnessed her work. I lowered the gas to almost total darkness, and asked her to thread her needle and proceed with her work, which she did at once, not seeming to notice that the room was darkened.

Anyway, her eyes were closed all during this time.

There is a theory that patients with this kind of syndrome may actually be mediumistic and be in the hands of malicious spirits who take them over and mistreat them. The occurrence of such supernormal activity as seeing in the dark and seeing with the eyes closed might be considered an indication of such a situation.

If ever there was a crazy, mixed-up kid, it was Miss Beauchamp, who is famous as the best observed and most successfully handled case of multiple personality—at least until Eve came along. Dr. Morton Prince, whom we have previously discussed, was her physician, and he reported every detail of her case in a book called *Dissociation of a Personality.*

Miss Beauchamp—why do they always choose such complicated pseudonyms? All those French names with accents and now Beauchamp, pronounced Beecham—came into therapy as a diligent and conscientious college student who was very unwilling to expose herself or her life to anybody's scrutiny. This dull personality was the only one known to her close friends. She was an individual of very high ideals and principles who suffered from neurasthenic aches and lack of vitality. She was reticent, extremely idealistic, and proud "to the point of morbidity." Hypnotherapy began in 1898, aimed at curing the neurasthenia, and some headway was made in this attempt. After the first few months, a personality appeared in hypnosis that denied having made certain statements in a previous trance state. This personality was saucy and irresponsible in contrast to the normal Miss Beauchamp —an altogether more interesting person. But let us give Prince the opportunity to tell about it ("Report to the International Congress of Psychology"):

The usual methods were employed with no result and it seemed as if Miss Beauchamp's case was hopeless. Finally I concluded to try hypnotic suggestions. She proved a very good subject, and the suggestions produced at the time rather brilliant results. In hypnosis she went easily into the somnambulistic state. This somnambulistic state came later to be known as B.II. while the first personality with whom I became acquainted, Miss Beauchamp herself, was known as B.I. Now I used to notice that as B.II, she was continually rubbing her eyes; her hands were in constant motion, always trying to get at her eyes. Still I paid very little attention to it, or placed very little significance in this fact, merely attributing it to nervousness. One day when I hypnotized her and referred to something that she had done in a previous state—that is to say, something that she had said or done in a previous state when I supposed she was B.II.—she denied all knowledge of it, and said it was not so. This surprised me, and I attributed the denial at first to an attempt at deception. Finally it turned out that when she went into the state of which she later denied the facts, she was an entirely distinct and separate person. This third personality, which then developed, came to be known as B.III.

B.III. was an interesting and quite remarkable personality, who was really a separate entity altogether from any of the Misses B. She insisted she was a spirit who had entered the body of Miss B. when they were both children and had become caught there and could not get away. She delighted in her opportunities to "get out" and exist in Miss B.'s body as a "real person" again.

Dr. Prince wrote:

One day, some time after this, when she was at home, owing to some nervous excitement she was thrown into the condition of B.III. and then, I not being there to prevent it, she rubbed her eyes until she got them opened, and from that time to this she (B.III.) has had a spontaneous and independent existence, and she always refers to events as being "before" or "after she got her eyes opened."

Now this personality came afterwards to be known as Sally. In character she differs very remarkably from B.I. . . . B.I. is a very serious-minded person, fond of books and study, of a religious turn of mind, and possesses a very morbid conscientiousness. Sally, on the other hand, if full of fun, does not worry about anything; all life is one great joke to her, she hates books, loves fun and amusement, does not like serious things, hates church, in fact is thoroughly childlike in every way. She is a child of nature. She insists, although of this I have no absolute proof, that she never sleeps, and that she is always awake while Miss Beauchamp is asleep. I believe it to be true. Then Miss Beauchamp is neurasthenic, Sally is perfectly well. She is never fatigued and never suffers pain. During the first year Sally and Miss Beauchamp used to come and go in succession. At first whenever B.I. became fatigued or upset from any cause, Sally was likely to come. The periods during which Sally was in existence might be any time from a few minutes to several hours. Later these periods became prolonged to several days. It must not be forgotten that though Miss Beauchamp knows nothing of Sally, Sally, when not in the flesh, is conscious of all Miss Beauchamp's thoughts and doings, and the latter could hide nothing from her. Curiously enough, Sally took an intense dislike to B.I. She actually hated her and there was no length to which she would not go to cause her annoyance. She would play every kind of prank on her to make her miserable. She tormented her to a degree almost incredible. While Sally would never do anything to make anyone else unhappy, she was absolutely remorseless in the way she tormented Miss Beauchamp by practical jokes and by playing upon her sensibilities. I will give a few illustrations. If there is one thing which Miss Beauchamp has a perfect horror of, it is snakes and spiders. They throw her into a condition of terror. One day Sally went out into the country and collected some snakes and spiders and put them into a little box. She brought them home and did them up in a little package, and addressed them to Miss Beauchamp, and when B.I. opened the package, they ran out and about the room and nearly sent her into fits. In order to get rid of them she had to handle them, which added to her terror.

A great friend of Miss Beauchamp, to whom she felt under strong obligations, had asked her to knit a baby's blanket. She worked on that blanket for nearly a year; as fast as she would get it near completion, Sally would unravel it, and then she would have to begin the task again, and regularly every time Sally would pull the whole thing to pieces. Finally she came to herself one day and found herself standing in the middle of the room tied up in a perfect network and snarl of worsted yarn; it was wound round the pictures and then round and round the furniture, the bed, the chairs, herself, and she had to cut it to get out of the snarl.

Miss Beauchamp is a person with a great sense of dignity, and dislikes anything that smacks of a lack of decorum or of familiarity. Sally has a way of punishing her by making her sit on a chair with her feet upon the mantelpiece. B.I. could not take her feet down, and was mortified to think she had to sit that way. Sally carries on a correspondence with Miss Beauchamp, writes letters to her pointing out all the weak points of her character, dwelling on all the little slips and foibles of her mind, telling her all the reckless acts and secret thoughts, indeed, everything she has done that won't bear criticism.

.   .   .

Although B.I. knows nothing of Sally, Sally is not only conscious of Miss Beauchamp's thoughts at the moment they arise, but she is capable, as I have said, of controlling her thoughts and her arms and legs and tongue to a certain extent. . . . During the time when Sally is in existence, B.I. is—as Sally puts it—"dead," and these times represent complete gaps in Miss Beauchamp's memory, and she has no knowledge of them whatever.

Sally, however, is never unconscious. Her memory is continuous. "The most remarkable part of Sally's personality, I think," says Prince

is that she has been able to write out for me her autobiography, beginning with the time when she was in her cradle, which she remembers. She actually describes her own thoughts and feelings as distinct from B.I.'s all through her childhood, up to and including the present time; although, as she says, she never got an independent existence until she "got her eyes open." She remembers her cradle, draws a picture of the bars in its sides, and remembers what she, as distinct from Miss Beauchamp, thought at the time when she was learning to walk. Then B.I. was frightened and wanted to go back, but Sally was not at all frightened and wanted to go ahead. She described B.I. as having had a butterfly mind as contrasted with her own. She, as a small child, disliked the things that B.I. liked, and vice versa. She describes her school life, her own feelings when B.I. did things, and the different sensations of the two selves when, for example, B.I. was punished and felt badly, and she herself was entirely indifferent and without remorse.

Prince, impressed as he was with the thought that Sally was Miss Beauchamp's unconscious mind and nothing more, would never for one moment have considered that she might be what she called herself, a spirit who had somehow become captured in the body and mind of another person. He says, gloatingly:

Thus I have been able to get *an actual autobiography of a subliminal consciousness, in which are described the contemporaneous and contrasted mental lives of two consciousnesses, the subliminal and the dominant, from early infancy to adult life.* In this Sally has described for me various scenes and incidents which occurred and which she saw during her early life, but of which Miss Beauchamp is entirely ignorant. These usually represent scenes which occurred when B.I. was absorbed in thought, but which Sally as a subliminal noticed. Taking all this into consideration—taking the present relations of Sally's thoughts to Miss Beauchamp's thought, and many other facts, like automatic writing, which Sally performs with ease, and uses for purposes of correspondence—I think we are safe in saying that *Sally is the subliminal consciousness,* which has become highly developed and organized and obtained finally an independent existence, and led an individual life of its own.

Later another personality became evident. This was called B.IV. She was of a very different character from either Sally or Miss Beauchamp—irritable, quick-tempered, and often quite unpleasant. Although Sally's mental life was also continuous during that of B.IV., and although she knew everything B.IV. did, at the time she did it, heard what she said, read what she wrote, and saw what she did, nevertheless *Sally did not know B.IV.'s thoughts.* For this reason Sally had great contempt for her and dubbed her "the Idiot." She transferred her hatred from B.I. to B.IV.

Prince particularly stressed one point: that however normal each of the personalities appeared, none was quite normal, as in each were missing some of the attributes of the original Miss Beauchamp—the one who existed before she underwent the various nervewracking experiences that had made her personality split. Eventually he was able to synthesize them all together—all except Sally. When this synthesis —the new or whole Miss Beauchamp—took over entirely, Sally had to leave. She went back, as she put it, "to where I came from." Wherever that was.

Prince concluded:

This final synthesis—the construction of what appears to be the original self—seems to me akin to proof of the correctness of the diagnosis.

15. Dangers and Misapprehensions

THERE IS AS MUCH conflicting information about the possible dangers of hypnosis as about every other phase of it. For every person who has a warning, there seems to be another who says it—whatever *it* is—is perfectly safe.

Dr. Bernard C. Gindes, for instance, in *New Concepts of Hypnosis*, comes on strong in favor of his pet argument:

Much of the fear propaganda promulgated around hypnosis has been built about the "dangers" of being unable to waken the subject. This is sheer nonsense, ignored by anyone with the slightest knowledge or experience of the science. If the subject is not awakened by the therapist, his state will automatically convert itself into natural sleep, from which he will waken naturally within an hour or so. . . . There has never been a case in all the annals of psychological history where a subject failed to return to a normal condition, despite the elaborate fancies of professional fictioneers.

I recall very clearly that in the fall of 1965 there was a continuing story in the newspapers for several weeks about a girl who had been hypnotized and just refused to return to normal consciousness. Apparently she had gone into an out-of-body experience—one of those mystical and magical things that are completely disregarded by most therapists as beneath the dignity of the profession—and she was so happy she just did not want to come back. Eventually, it is to be hoped, she did wake up at the command, but it would be doubtful if her hypnotist ever took the chance of putting her into trance again.

Another who insistently decrees that there is no danger is Leslie LeCron, a psychologist who has specialized in the study of hypnosis. In his booklet *Self-Hypnosis,* he says: "Many people think that a hypnotized person will carry out any suggestion given to him. This is nonsense. No one will do anything under hypnosis that he is not ordinarily willing to do. Suggestions must be acceptable to *both* the conscious and subconscious parts of the mind." Others say the same thing, just as emphatically.

However, the number of actual cases that refute this are legion. A. Cannon in a piece titled "Hypnosis in Criminology" in the *British Journal of Medical Hypnotism* cites an experiment by Liegeois in which a Mrs. G—— was told to kill a Mr. M——. A revolver was given her, and at the appointed time she stepped up to him and, as she thought, shot him. Taken before a police commissioner, she acknowledged the crime, emphatically denied that she had acted under the influence of any suggestion, and declared herself perfectly ready to suffer for her deed, being convinced that she saw Mr. M——'s body lying bleeding before her.

Cannon also refers to several other reports of early cases

involving sex crimes committed upon hypnotized young ladies, one involving a Marseilles hypnotist in 1858 and another a Rouen dentist. An Associated Press account of April 1, 1949, stated that in Martinez, California, a man was convicted of rape upon a woman who had been hypnotized against her will.

To get someone to do something under hypnosis he would not normally do, it is a matter of convincing him that he is doing something else or that what he is doing is essential. Most writers on the subject assert quite definitely that no one under hypnosis may be induced to do anything offensive to his moral sensibilities. "On the other hand," says Samuel Glasner in "Social Psychological Aspects of Hypnosis," "there are a few courageous spirits who have dared to challenge this general consensus. They point out that this begs the question, because should hypnotic or posthypnotic suggestion succeed in producing an antisocial act, it would be taken as evidence of the subject's lack of morals, rather than of the effectiveness of hypnosis."

In *Hypnotism*, J. Albert Moll minimized the danger of hypnotism being used for criminal purposes, but nevertheless he told this story on himself: "I reported to the Society of Prussian Medical Officers a case of a man who in the posthypnotic state promised a donation to the Society, and carefully explained in writing that he did it of his own accord, after I had suggested to him that he should think so."

Moll also supplied quite an impressive list of ways in which hypnotism might be used for criminal purposes. These include:

1. Assault of the subject by the hypnotist—seduction the most likely crime here.

2. The posthypnotic production of some functional difficulty such as paralysis.

3. The production of abortion through hypnotic suggestion.

4. Causing an individual to commit suicide.

5. Murder by arousing the emotionality of the subject to the point of overworking his heart.

6. Securing illegal possession of property through posthypnotic suggestion in reference to signing wills or other legal papers.

7. The production of false testimony by causing the subject to have hallucinations that he accepts as real or by suggestion to cause a falsification of memory.

Then it might also be possible by hypnotic or posthypnotic suggestion to cause the subject to harm someone else or to harm himself. And Glasner supplements Moll's list by suggesting also the implanting in the subject of mean or obnoxious thoughts and attitudes, thus producing undesirable personality traits.

What is perhaps the first case of a murderer being exonerated because he committed a crime in a hypnotic trance happened in 1951 in Copenhagen. There were two important points in this case. For one thing, the court recognized that the responsibility rested only with the hypnotist. For another, the mastermind was able to control his mental slave because he knew something about him that made the prospective murderer feel guilty—their mutual collaboration with the enemy during the war.

On March 29, 1951, a young man dressed in blue worker's overalls entered the Landmands Bank, walking stiffly like a mechanical toy soldier wound up by a key. He held up the bank, killed two persons who resisted, and ran away without the money he had asked for. His motorcycle was followed, and when he was apprehended and questioned it was learned that his name was Pelle Hardrup. He confessed to the crime, saying he was guilty; he had done just as his good angel told him to. When he was asked who his good angel was, he repeated always the same answer: "I cannot tell."

Later an ex-convict came to the police and said that he had been in prison with Pelle and a man named Björn Nielsen. "It all goes back to politics—old Nazi politics," he said. Then he told that while they were in jail, Nielsen had constantly hypnotized Pelle and had so conditioned him that whenever he saw an X he would go into hypnotic sleep and obey Nielsen's commands. "During our days and months in prison he was a walking doll, a zombie who obeyed Nielsen blindly with no will of his own," the man said.

Pelle was apparently never out of trance long enough to come to himself and clear himself of the charges of bank robbery and murder. Even when he was put in jail for them, Nielsen paid another prisoner to make Xs on the walls, and constantly sent him letters in which there were numerous Xs. Finally Pelle's wife, who had been afraid to talk, confessed all she knew about the hold Nielsen had over her husband, and Pelle was placed in solitary confinement so that Nielsen could not possibly get at him. There he would not eat or move until about the fifth day, when he called the guard, his eyes staring feverishly from their sockets. He asked for food, paper, and a pen; when he received them he wrote the entire night. His statement, presented in court along with the testimony of his wife and others, was enough to exonerate him of the crimes. The report by Kurt Singer ("Murder by Hypnosis," *Tomorrow*, Autumn 1959) does not tell the outcome; but Simeon Edmunds in *Hypnotism and E.S.P.* states: "Nielsen was convicted of murder and imprisoned for life. Hardrup was found guilty but not responsible for his actions, and was sent to a psychiatric hospital."

Psychiatrist Joost A. M. Meerloo says in the *Parapsychology Review* (March–April 1970): "Several textbooks on hypnosis inform us that the patient's superego is strong enough to protect him against immoral suggestions given in a trance. Experimental hypnosis has shown that this is not the case. The art of moral seduction is based on repeated fragmentized suggestions that gradually permit the other party to give in to what he or she would never have done without those repeated suggestions." Dr. Meerloo adds: "It is a scientific fairy tale to believe nobody can be hypnotized against his will."

A laboratory experiment undertaken by L. W. Rowland was reported in "Will Hypnotized Persons Try to Harm Themselves or Others?" (*Journal of Abnormal Social Psychology*, 1939). The experiments were designed to test two hypotheses: that subjects under hypnosis may be induced to perform actions that are dangerous to themselves and that they would not perform when not in the hypnotic state; and that subjects under hypnosis may be induced to perform actions harmful to other people, which they would not perform in their normal state.

Rowland made a large box shielded by a sheet of plate glass bent in such a way that reflections were removed and the glass was totally invisible. A large rattlesnake was then placed in the box. Using four previously trained hypnotic subjects, Rowland hypnotized them deeply and then instructed two of them: "There is a piece of coiled rubber rope in that box. Go up to the box, reach through the screen wire, and pick it up." One of the subjects walked to the box but awoke out of the trance when he saw the snake. The other attempted to reach in for the "rope" but was prevented by the invisible glass.

With two other subjects, Rowland, after hypnotizing them, stated frankly to them: "There is a rattlesnake in that box. Go up to it and reach through the opening in the screen wire and pick up the snake." Both subjects attempted to comply with his instructions and were only protected by the glass.

In a second experiment Rowland used two other subjects who were instructed, under hypnosis, to throw a glass of sulphuric acid at Rowland's face, which was protected by the invisible glass. Both subjects complied, although one of them was greatly disturbed afterward.

Rowland therefore concluded—and who could blame him?—that persons in deep hypnosis will allow themselves to be exposed to unreasonably dangerous situations and will perform acts unreasonably dangerous to others.

W. R. Wells in "Experiment in the Hypnotic Production of Crime" told a previously trained subject, whom he called Yo, that if hypnotized he would be made to perform a criminal act, and then hypnotized him over his conscious resistance. Then he gave Yo a posthypnotic suggestion that after coming out of hypnosis he would go to Wells's overcoat and take a dollar bill. He would think these were his own coat and his own money. Then he would have amnesia about the act, and when he discovered the bill in his own pocket he would remember (falsely) that he'd had this extra dollar when he came to the office.

The results of the experiment were successful at every point. In front of several fellow students Yo did everything he had been told, insisted it was his own coat and his own money, argued with those who suggested it was not.

An interesting series of tests were performed on military personnel by J. G Watkins and reported in "Antisocial Compulsions Induced Under Hypnotic Trance." He hypnotized a corporal, to whom a captain had previously given some secret military information that the corporal was certain he could not be made to reveal to anyone else. After placing him in trance, Watkins said to him: "I am Captain X. I just gave you a piece of information you were not to divulge. I want to see if you remember it, Corporal. What is it?" The subject divulged the information with posthypnotic amnesia for having done so.

In another experiment Watkins hypnotized a private and told him that in a minute he would open his eyes and see a Japanese soldier in front of him. "He has a bayonet and is going to kill you unless you kill him first. You will have to strangle him with your bare hands." A lieutenant colonel, the head psychiatrist, on whom a private would not dare lay violent hands under ordinary circumstances, was placed directly in front of the subject about ten feet away. The subject opened his eyes, then began to creep cautiously forward. Suddenly, in a flying tackle he dove at the colonel, knocking him against the wall, and with both of his hands began strangling him. It must be noted that the man did not violate his own conscience. He was attacking an aggressive enemy and not an Army officer. He could easily have murdered him under that false belief had he not been forcibly restrained.

These researchers proved that people could be hypnotized against their wills, despite their conscious resistance. The corporal involved in the above experiment had been previously hypnotized and told he would immediately go to sleep upon being handed a yellow pencil. He was now offered a ten dollar bill if he could resist going to sleep. However, as soon as he was handed the yellow pencil, he went into trance.

A nurse in a psychiatric hospital who had previously shown herself to be an excellent subject insisted that she could not be hypnotized against her will. Watkins sat her at a desk and placed a dollar bill in front of her. Then he told her, before witnesses: "You can have this money if you will keep from entering trance regardless of what I say or do." She said: "You didn't place any limitations on the way in which I could resist you so I'm going to close my eyes, plug up my ears, and constantly talk and shout loudly so that I can't hear anything you say." This she did, while the experimenter strongly and firmly repeated, close to her ear: "My voice will gradually reach you and you will hear it in spite of your shouting. You will begin to feel very uncomfortable. There will be a pain in your head which will grow and grow. It becomes stronger, much stronger. After a while it will become excruciating. It will be unbearable, and everything in you will cry out for relief. But the only way out of this intense pain will be to enter a deep sleep."

The subject fought valiantly, although she soon began to hold her head and exclaim: "My God but it hurts"; but then she would continue her shouts of defiance. At the end of six minutes she suddenly stopped her shouting, tossed the dollar bill at the experimenter, and said: "Here, take it." She immediately slumped in her chair in a deep trance.

A psychiatrist who observed the experiment not only confirmed the results but herself became emotionally indignant, exclaiming: "Why, that's virtually rape. If anybody did that to me I could kill them."

The subject later said that the headache had become so

unbearable that nothing, not even a million dollars, could have induced her to resist the suggestions any longer. Later, at her request, she was rehypnotized and given posthypnotic suggestions to the effect that she could never again be hypnotized by anyone unless she chose voluntarily to cooperate.

Which leads us to another danger that has apparently not been thought of by any of those who write about it. What if the hypnotist who told a subject he had a terrible headache or he could not pull his hands apart, took that moment to drop dead? Would it leave a permanently handicapped subject? Some of the things we have mentioned in this book that professors have done to their pupils would be pretty traumatic if the subjects were left that way. And even hypnotists do die suddenly on occasion, do they not?

We have talked a lot here about posthypnotic suggestion. It is the term applied to a command made while the subject is entranced, but that is to be carried out after he awakes. Sometimes an interval of months may elapse between the command and its fulfillment. Almost invariably, at the stated time the suggestion is obeyed, the recipient is perhaps unaware of the source of his impulse, not finding adequate logical grounds for the action he performs; or perhaps he automatically lapses into the hypnotic state. It is interesting how he will then attempt to rationalize his actions.

Norman Lobsenz, in his article in *Good Housekeeping*, said: "A person carrying out posthypnotic suggestion—taking off a shoe, for instance—may say to the hypnotist, 'I knew you *wanted* me to do that.' At other times the subject will go to great lengths to find 'logical' reasons for his action. He might explain carefully that his sock was bunched up, or a corn hurt, or he wanted to check the shoe size." In one test Lobsenz reports on a man who was told he would think he was God. When he awoke from his trance and said he was God, the hypnotist replied, "I don't doubt that, but tell me, how exactly did you create the universe?" "God" was stumped, but only briefly. Then he resolved his problem triumphantly with the statement, "God never talks shop."

Hypnosis is not dependable in crime detection or lie detector tests, just because of this kind of rationalization. Dr. Harold Rosen, chairman of the committee on hypnosis of the A.M.A. Council on Mental Health, says that he has been asked by police and lawyers to hypnotize suspects to "get the truth," but he realizes it can't be done. "A hypnotized person may confess to a crime he committed only in fantasy, or to please the hypnotist. He may distort, lie, or tell what he *thinks* happened," says Dr. Rosen.

Damaging "admissions" can be suggested into a subject's mind. One man confessed to murdering his sister, even though he did not have a sister, says Lobsenz.

If there are problems that occur when professional hypnotists are at work, think of the dangers when laymen attempt it! The feeling of assurance that is essential to being a good hypnotist and the air of competence he must exude, may impress a subject into believing that he knows much more about what he is doing than he actually does. A friend of mine named Renée was once hypnotized by such an individual, who thought he was quite adequate but was sadly misinformed about himself.

Because of poltergeistlike activity in her home after she had bought at auction the picture of a seventeenth-century Dutch gentleman, Renée, a believer in possible contact with the spirit world, decided that the old fellow must have accompanied his picture to her home. She called him by the name Kuvoort and felt his presence with her at all times. She then decided that if she were hypnotized into a mediumistic trance, he might speak through her and tell why he was there and what was going on with him. And so a session was held, and Kuvoort was invited to attend. He apparently did, for as soon as Renée was entranced, she began to speak in a deep voice with a Dutch accent. The entire conversation was taped. I have heard it and been amused, but what happened to Renée wasn't funny at all.

As Kuvoort talked he continually asked for "schnapps." There was no gin in the house, nor even beer, so he was asked if brandy would do, and he agreed. All during the long interview he was given brandy every time he called for schnapps—and that was often. He imbibed so much that he gradually began to slur his words as he talked and to be more and more boisterous.

Renée, whose system could stand no more than one, or two at the most, shots of brandy before she became intoxicated, was having a fantastic amount of booze poured into her. Being asleep, she was not aware what the old Dutchman was doing to her; and, apparently even less alert, the hypnotist did not know what was going on either. When the discussion was over, he awoke Renée precipitously, saying nothing that might help her body to cope with the unfortunate situation. So he returned to consciousness a lady so drunk that she was ill for days.

Another danger of hypnosis was revealed when Veryl Smith of Salt Lake City, Utah observed the reactions of a friend who was highly suggestible. He was also quite mediumistic and subject to going into trance, and thus had no proper protection against the suggestions of a hypnotist, or even those for self-hypnosis. As Veryl described it to me:

A few days ago a friend and I put a record "Sounds of Self-Hypnosis Through Relaxation" on the record player and stretched out, he on a folded blanket on the floor and I on the couch, to listen and follow the suggestions without a preliminary hearing, as the hypnotist on the record recommended.

I achieved a very pleasant sense of relaxation and well being. I was aware of all that went on—a distant phone ringing, my friend's deep breathing as the hypnotist counted to ten, etc. I was aware that my friend must have achieved a rather deep level of hypnosis for at the second set of ten deep breaths he was not following the counting. His breaths were very heavy and long. When the wake-up suggestion was given I sat up and watched as my friend struggled to come back to reality. He seemed unable to orientate himself or to remember what had happened. At last he got to his feet, folded the blanket and remarked that he was stiff and a little cold from being on the floor and wished he could relax. Immediately as he said the word relax he slumped to the floor, and stretched out in a deep sleep. I had heard that a subject under hypnosis would eventually fall into normal sleep and awaken from this if undisturbed, so I did nothing, and after awhile he did awaken, remembering very little of what had happened.

As I told him what had taken place he was sitting backward on a chair, facing me, with his arms folded over the back. When I told him what had happened when he had spoken the word "relax," he went out again . . . at the instant I spoke the word, with his head down on his arms and breathing deeply. Not wishing to wait for him to awaken naturally this time, I told him he would wake up when I counted to five and be alert and normal. He did awake readily on the count of five and I again had to tell him what had happened, since he didn't even remember that we had played the record. I told him it had offered a key word for the subject to use to reestablish the state achieved while listening to the recording and that we had already used this word twice by accident, throwing him into deep sleep each time, and that we must avoid using it again. I had to explain it all to him and to warn him not to leave the house, for he often tells himself to relax, especially while driving the fifty to one hundred miles in heavy traffic required each day on his job.

At first he didn't believe what I was telling him; but finally he shook his head and said, "Well, the record must have really made me relax. . . ." and again for the third time, he instantly fell asleep. I now realized I'd have to handle the situation alone and somehow reverse the "relax" suggestion. I talked to him, telling him that from then on the suggestion made by the recording regarding the word relax would have no further effect, and that the word would have only the usual everyday meaning for him. Then I awakened him with a count of five and nearly wept with relief when I spoke the word and saw that it no longer had any effect on him. He could not remember anything that had happened involving it.

We were very much concerned with the dangers inherent in such recordings, since no provision was made that could safeguard the subject from an experience such as my friend had. What if it had happened while he was driving his car or operating machinery? Of course, we realized that it is a rare person who would be so bothered. And yet just such unusual subjects are the ones who would be most likely to be interested in playing self-hypnotic records.

All professional and medical hypnotists warn against lay use of this potent force, to little avail because it is so easy that anyone with sufficient self-assurance can attempt it, frequently successfully. Unfortunately, many such experimenters are using hypnosis as a psychical plaything.

There is a story going around, and I cannot verify it for truthfulness, that the recent subject of a book about age regression to a past life has herself been taken over by the personality whom she role-played. (This is not the famous Bridey Murphy case, by the way. I am not discussing it here because so much has already been published about it.) But another girl who gave a slight amount of evidence about an ostensible past life is said now to be living that role constantly, instead of her own present life. To those who believe reincarnation is the only answer, she is reliving the past in a detrimental way. To those who believe in the possibility of spirit possession, she evidently went into a mediumistic trance the first time she was age regressed, and an entity spoke through her just as Kuvoort did through Renée. If this was the case, then the entity has apparently moved in on the girl and is possessing her. This is tragic and should not have been allowed to happen. As long as we persist in refusing to face up to the possibility of a life of continuity after death, there is the chance that some of the evidence for it will be misinterpreted, and thus proper care to avoid disaster will not be taken. This danger must be faced eventually, and surely the time is not far away.

Also what about the psychologist who bravely and brashly undertakes the rehabilitation of a split personality, aware he is on unsure ground, but completely unwilling to consider the possibilities of certain areas in which he refuses to believe? If he runs into another Sally, as Dr. Prince did, will he be fortunate enough always to be able to send her "back to where she came from"?

There is no doubt that the medical profession is well aware of the dangers of hypnosis. But primarily for others, not for themselves, it would seem. Even so, the first and oldest organization of medical hypnotists in this country, the Society for Clinical and Experimental Hypnosis, recommends at least a year of training for any doctor or dentist who wants to use hypnosis in his specialty. It fears some doctors will try hypnosis after only a cursory course and, unaware of its limitations, will do more harm than good.

Dr. Milton V. Kline, editor of the society's journal, warns: "Quickie courses give the men the tool but not the appreciation of how carefully it must be used." He points to the case of a patient who came to him after having been hypnotized by a dentist. The dentist had stopped the man from grinding his teeth; but he was neurotic. When he could no longer find a teeth-grinding outlet for his tensions, he started to overeat. When he came to Kline his weight had soared from 145 pounds to 288 pounds.

Also, in other areas, doctors may be pressured into using hypnosis unwisely. As its applications become more and more varied there is danger that the public will take to hypnosis as heedlessly as it has to tranquilizers. To avoid this, Southwestern Medical School in Dallas permits hypnosis only after the case is discussed at a conference of several different specialists.

Dr. Harold B. Crasilneck advises (*Life*, March 7, 1960) that hypnosis "should be used only with specific cases that no longer respond to standard treatment." Some doctors do not heed this advice. Having used hypnosis to relieve physical distress during a patient's ulcer operation, for instance, a too ambitious doctor may try to get at the psychosomatic reasons for the ulcer. Unless he is grounded in clinical psychology, Crasilneck warns, he can botch this and drive the patient into hysteria.

Dr. George Estabrooks, an American authority on the subject, reported in *Hypnotism* a case told him by a doctor friend whose patient complained of the delusion of being followed by a large black dog. He said it had been going on for several days, and he had been unable to throw it off. The doctor soon elicited the fact that the patient had volunteered to be the subject at a show by a stage hypnotist and had been put into a deep trance, after which he remembered nothing of what had taken place during the performance. When inquiries were made from the patient's friends who had accompanied him to the show, it was learned that, when hypnotized, he had caused much amusement by running around the stage pursued by an imaginary black dog. It was necessary for the patient to be hypnotized several times before the posthypnotic suggestion, which presumably had been accidentally and unintentionally left by the stage hypnotist, could be removed.

When it is realized that such instances as this are not infrequent, there is little wonder that physicians view with considerable alarm the stage magician who puts members of his audience into trance. Both physical and mental harm can come from his act, says the American Medical Association. "The use of hypnosis for entertainment purposes," the A.M.A. flatly declared, "is vigorously condemned." Medical hypnotists hope state governments will pass bills banning hypnosis in the amusement field, but the opposition from entertainers is powerful. In 1957 the city council of Buffalo, New York considered such a resolution. It was opposed by Ring Twelve of the Buffalo Magic Club on the grounds of discrimination and quietly dropped.

Life says: "Unfortunately, healing by untrained hypnotists flourishes in the nation today and the situation is getting worse now that hypnosis is medically respectable. Many reputable hypnotists now warn their sleeping patients: 'You will never under any condition allow yourself to be hypnotized by anyone who is not qualified to do so.'"

The question here is, who is qualified? Does anyone really know enough about the subject to be able safely to experiment with it? When you are working with the human mind you are dealing with the most important thing in the world. Handle it carefully.

16. Mesmerism Revisited

THERE HAVE ALWAYS continued to be a few people with the vague suspicion that there was, perhaps, something beyond hypnotism and suggestion, and this caused them to reconsider the idea of mesmerism. A twentieth-century researcher who became convinced of the efficacy of mesmerism was French Dr. Emile Boirac, rector of the Dijon Academy. He said in *Psychic Science*, published in 1918: "Certain attitudes and maneuvers have, by themselves and independently of all suggestion, the property of benumbing the nervous centers and producing sleep." These he believed, were the result of mesmerism.

In the early 1900s, when Boirac was formulating his theories, he says that all doctors and savants who were engaged in the study of hypnosis were strongly inclined to think with Bernheim that suggestion is the key to all the phenomena, or even that "there is no hypnotism, there is only suggestion." But Boirac was sure that there were suggestible *and* mesmeric subjects.

"For my part," he said, "I have known at least five (and the total number of persons with whom I have experimented is not considerable) who possessed this remarkable property" of being sensitive not only to suggestion but to mesmerism. He believed that he eliminated the possibility of suggestion from his techniques because "when experimenting with them, I have always taken the precaution of bandaging the eyes hermetically, without saying a word or permitting any of the sitters to break the silence throughout the duration of the experiments. Further, in the majority of cases, I have allowed them to remain awake, doing nothing to modify the condition of their brain." All he ever said to them was: "Will you kindly allow me to put on this bandage; sit there, and when you think you feel anything, will you please tell me?" Under these conditions he "obtained the most varied and precise effects in all parts of their bodies corresponding with the position and movements of my own right hand or left, placed opposite the various parts." He was convinced that "certain attitudes and maneuvers have, by themselves and independently of all suggestion, the property of benumbing the nervous centers and producing sleep; that seems to us to be as certain, although as little explained, as the soporific efficacy of opium."

For example, he said:

For six months I had had a young Pyrenean of fifteen years of age as servant—Jean M.—of extreme hypnotic sensibility; and the following are the notes which I took of experiments carried out with this subject.

I have only to place my open hand behind his elbow or any part of his body in order rapidly to bring about jerks, movements, etc. and that, so far as I can judge, without anything telling him of my action, whilst he has his back turned to me, is engaged in reading, talking, etc. Several times when he was asleep naturally, it was sufficient for me to extend my hand over him, at a distance of five or six inches, to see his chest expand, rise, as though drawn by my hand as it rose, and fall back when the distance became too great. Magnetic influence perhaps, but also perhaps, the simple phenomenon of hyperesthesia of touch.

But Boirac then began to have even more interesting results. On a Sunday afternoon, looking into the boy's room, he found him lying fully dressed on his bed. He decided to make a mesmeric experiment:

Standing on the landing at a distance of about three yards, I extended my right hand in his direction and at the height of his feet. . . . After one or two minutes, or probably even less, I slowly raised my hand, and to my great astonishment, I saw the sleeper's feet rise together by a muscular contraction which began at the knees and follow the ascending movement of my hand in the air. I repeated the experiment three times and the phenomenon was reproduced three times with the regularity and precision of a physical phenomenon. Amazed, I went in search of Mme. Boirac, asking her to make as little noise as possible.

On his return with his wife, he found that the sleeper had not moved. He repeated the manifestation. "Try to do it by thought," suggested his wife. So "I fixed my eyes on his feet and they slowly rose. Incredible! The feet followed the movements of my eyes, rising, stopping and descending with them."

When his wife had her hand on his, she was able also to have the same success with the sleeper. But when she ceased to touch her husband, there was no result.

After this, Boirac naturally had a desire to attempt hypnosis at a distance whenever he could. One day he went to the Casino about noon to have some coffee and to listen to the rehearsal of a small orchestra. There were seats for customers and a long terrace where people came every day to play cards. As he sipped his coffee, he saw a subject of his, Dockmann, sitting in the garden with a friend who was reading a newspaper; his back was almost turned to Boirac, and he began to roll a cigarette. The idea came to the doctor to try to mesmerize his subject at a distance.

"Concentrating my mind entirely on this one thought," he writes

I looked steadfastly in Dockmann's direction, and commanded him to stop all movements and go to sleep. Dockmann did not appear to perceive that I was looking at him, but his actions quickly slackened, and his eyes became fixed. The unfinished cigarette remained in his hands, he suddenly dropped his eyelids, and became motionless as a statue. His friend raised his head, perceived his condition, questioned him, but obtained no response. A singer seated at a neighboring table became frightened and screamed aloud. I hastened and went down, and in a few moments, by breathing quickly on his eyes, awoke my improvised subject, who did not even seem to know what had happened to him.

On the following day he repeated the act with the same innocent Dockmann, who was sitting quietly at a table by himself writing a letter. Boirac says: "I again concentrated myself with a nervous tension, which caused me to vibrate from head to foot, and, while looking quietly at Dockmann, I commanded him with all my power to cease writing and go to sleep." The reaction was slower than the day before, but he soon went under.

Another subject, Gustave P——, was just as susceptible.

Once the two of them were in Boirac's den sitting before the fire.

Without looking at him, my eyes being fixed in the direction of the fireplace, I mentally commanded him to go to sleep, with all the will power of which I was capable, and in less than a minute . . . raising my eyes towards him, I saw that he was asleep. . . . I asked him why he had gone to sleep without my permission; he told me that he had suddenly felt the same heat and disturbance in his head which always preceded the sleep which I provoked.

On another occasion "I had asked Gustave to meet me at my house about three o'clock. After he had been in my study a few minutes he asked me to give him something to drink. I went out of the room to give the order for some beer to be brought, and through the door I mentally commanded him to go to sleep. When I opened the door I found him asleep. I mentally awaked him and we resumed our conversation as though nothing had happened."

So what was going on here? It was obviously this same telepathy at a distance we have run into before. Boirac preferred to think of it as mental suggestion, but he liked to argue with current concepts about it.

I do not know if mental suggestion exists; for my part I have never succeeded in provoking this phenomenon except under the form of sending to sleep and awakening provoked by a simple mental command; but if mental suggestion exists it is not a phenomenon of suggestion, it is a phenomenon of magnetism. Do not let us be deceived by words; the pretended mental suggestion, a very unfortunate name, has nothing in common with suggestion properly so called. . . . The whole mystery resides in this influence that one brain exercises at a distance on another. But who does not see that this influence is just a particular instance of magnetic influence in general? Instead of supposing that this influence radiates from all parts of a living body, we suppose that it radiates exclusively from one brain to another. If, therefore, the phenomena which I have described can be explained by mental suggestion, that amounts to saying that in the main they can be explained by animal magnetism, because I imagine that we do not attribute to thought and will the mystical property of communicating themselves from one mind to another without any physical connection between the brains in which they have their material conditions.

Of course today we have an entirely different idea about telepathy, suspecting that it does *not* involve any physical connection from one mind to another. But we do not really know much more about it *for sure* than we did in Boirac's day.

Magnetism is still being used, although seldom is it occupied with putting people to sleep at a distance. Some persons prefer the deeper sleep brought about by passes to the lighter ones that occur when just suggestion is used.

Leslie LeCron said in "Hypnosis in the Production of Psi Phenomena" (*International Journal of Parapsychology,* Summer 1961):

One of the important parts of . . . the success with ESP during mesmeric trance is that the old time mesmerists as a rule took a long time for their inductions. Undoubtedly, this produced a far deeper state of trance than is customarily seen today. Modern operators seldom take more than fifteen or twenty minutes for the induction process. As Esdaile described his methods, he often spent anywhere from an hour to four or five hours of continued induction, using the passes.

Today these mesmeric passes are rarely used, though one psychiatrist, Dr. Edith Klemperer of New York has reported using them and finding the trance she induces deeper than when mere suggestion is used. Today, passes are merely regarded as an indirect suggestion. If the subject thinks they will produce hypnosis, he then slips into a trance as a result of the expectation of doing so. I know of no scientific tests ever made with adequate controls to ascertain whether the hypnotic trance is the same or differs from the mesmeric trance produced by passes.

The famous author Aldous Huxley asked Laura Archera, shortly after he met her, if she had ever attempted magnetic passes. When this woman who was to become his second wife said she had not, he replied: "You must try them sometime— they are effective and disreputable—just like dianetics."

In *This Timeless Moment*, the book she wrote about the last days of her husband's life, Laura quotes his own statement about the death of his first wife, Maria, and how he helped make it easier by the use of both hypnosis and mesmeric passes. Aldous wrote:

I spent a good many hours of each day sitting with her, sometimes saying nothing, sometimes speaking. When I spoke, it was always, first of all, to give suggestions about her physical well-being. I would go through the ordinary procedure of hypnotic induction, beginning by suggestions of muscular relaxation, then counting to five or ten, with the suggestion that each count would send her deeper into hypnosis. I would generally accompany the counting with passes of the hand, which I drew slowly down from the head towards the feet. After the induction period was over, I would suggest that she was feeling, and would continue to feel, comfortable, free from pain and nausea, desirous of taking water and liquid nourishment whenever they should be offered. These suggestions were, I think, effective; at any rate there was little pain and it was only during the last thirty-six hours that sedation . . . became necessary.

These suggestions for physical comfort were in every case followed by a much longer series of suggestions addressed to the deeper levels of the mind. Under hypnosis Maria had had, in the past, many remarkable visionary experiences of a kind which theologians would call "pre-mystical." She had also had . . . a number of genuinely mystical experiences, had lived with an abiding sense of divine immanence, of Reality totally present, moment by moment in every object, person and event.

. . .

Addressing the deep mind which never sleeps, I went on suggesting that there should be relaxation on the physical level, and an absence of pain and nausea; and I continued to remind her of who she really was—a manifestation in time of eternal, a part forever unseparated from the whole, of the divine reality; I went on urging her to go forward into the light.

17. Hypnosis and Dreams

IF PSYCHOTHERAPISTS COULD understand more about interpreting the content of dreams, especially by experimentally controlling them, they possibly could be more helpful to their patients. And if parapsychologists knew how to control dreaming, they might have a useful tool for devising ESP testing. While using hypnosis in some of their experimentation, however, none of them have ever resorted to such expedients to incite dreams as were reported by James Braid.

Some doctors in Braid's time apparently on occasion used the method of whispering in patients' ears in order to control their dreaming. In discussing this, Braid refers to a rather unsophisticated case recorded by a Dr. Abercrombie, on the authority of a Dr. Gregory—that of an officer in the expedition to Louisburgh in 1758. Braid says that having found how suggestible this chap was, his fellow officers were in the habit of amusing themselves at his expense. They could produce any kind of dream they chose, especially if the whispering was done by one with whose voice he was familiar. "Thus," said Braid,

at one time they conducted him through the whole process of a quarrel, ending in a duel; and when it was supposed the parties met, a pistol was put in his hand, which he fired, and was awakened by its report.

On another occasion, being asleep on the locker of the cabin, he was made to believe that he had fallen overboard, and was told to save himself by swimming. He imitated the art of swimming, when they told him to dive for his life, as a shark was pursuing him, which he attempted so energetically that he threw himself from the locker, by which he bruised himself severely. Again, after the landing of the army, he was found one day asleep in his tent, and apparently much annoyed with the noise of the cannonading then going on briskly. He was made to believe he was engaged with the enemy, when he expressed much fear, and betrayed a wish to run away. They remonstrated against this act of cowardice, whilst they increased his alarm by imitating the groans of the wounded; and when he inquired who was killed, which he often did, they named his particular friends. At last he was told that the man next him in the line had fallen, when he instantly sprang from his bed, rushed out of the tent, and was aroused from his sleep, and relieved from his fears, by falling over the tent ropes. It is added that after these experiments he had no distinct recollection of his dreams, but only a confused feeling of oppression or fatigue; and used to say to his friends that he was sure they had been playing him some tricks.

Various investigators have presented data to support the contention that hypnotically-induced dreams include symbolizations, distortions, and other characteristics of the "dream-work" and are in general indistinguishable from spontaneous night dreams. Dr. Theodore X. Barber, in a survey titled

"Toward a Theory of 'Hypnotic' Behavior: The 'Hypnotically Induced Dream'" (*Journal of Nervous and Mental Diseases*, 1962), critically reviewed various work that has been done along related lines. I will not attempt to go into this report deeply, but a few interesting points were brought out that might help us to understand the involvement of hypnotism with dreaming.

From the University of Texas Bulletin (1930), D. B. Klein's subjects were told in hypnotic sleep: "I want you to watch carefully for any dreams you may have and as soon as the dream is over tell me all about it." While the subject waited for a dream to appear, an external stimulus was introduced. Immediately following the stimulus, the hypnotized subject reported imaginative productions that they termed dreams. The author presented the following illustrative examples:

1. Stimulus: Right hand stroked with cotton for a few seconds. Dream report: "A cow licked me on the hand."
2. Stimulus: Bottle of asafetida held to the nose for ten seconds. Dream report: "Smelled something dead—a horse—a dead horse."

All dreams presented by Klein's hypnotized subjects were similar to the above, seemingly consisting of brief and unelaborated thoughts and images. However, subjects agreed that the experiences could be termed dreams, and the author concluded that since hypnotic dreams deal with events that subjects regard as really taking place at the time of the experience, they belong "in the same category of mental processes as the ordinary night dream."

More interesting dreams were occasionally found when the investigators attempted to elicit symbolic dreaming from hypnotized subjects. G. Roffenstein did not have much luck with this from a number of hypnotized subjects, but finally succeeded with a twenty-eight-year-old uneducated domestic worker. She was given the following suggestions under hypnosis: "You will dream of masturbation, rape, intercourse, etc. but you must dream this so, distort the dream so, hide its contents so, that the dream will seem entirely innocuous." Upon energetic repetition and reiterated explanation of these suggestions, she produced symbolic hypnotic dreams such as the following: When given the suggestion to dream of rape, she reported a dream in which she was attacked by a dog that tore at her throat; when given the suggestion to dream of masturbation, she reported dreaming of eating candy in bed.

Another symbolic dream was reported by M. Mazer in "An Experimental Study of the Hypnotic Dream." When instructed to dream symbolically about the female breast, one subject dreamt of a young boy walking barefoot over a very soft feather quilt. (He must obviously have heard that joke about "an acre of them to walk over barefoot.")

Barber concluded: "The 'hypnotized' subject purposively creates, 'makes up,' or tries to think of symbols which indirectly represent the suggested dream topic. Carefully controlled experiments are needed to confirm or disprove these hypotheses."

Dr. Charles Tart of the University of California at Davis, one of the leading authorities on out-of-body experiences, has also done dream studies. In "The Control of Nocturnal Dreaming by Means of Posthypnotic Suggestion" (*International Journal of Parapsychology*, Autumn 1967), he says:

Dream research has been almost exclusively a matter of correlational research using the EEG (electroencephalogram) and rapid eye movement (REM) technique. Researchers ask subjects how often they dreamed in color, whether their dreams were mainly pleasant or unpleasant, etc., and then attempted to correlate these observed characteristics with personality traits, intelligence, age, etc. Or a patient brought in a spontaneous dream and the therapist-researcher attempted to "interpret" it in the light of what he knew about the patient.

. . .

If we could gain active control over the content and process of nocturnal dreaming we could learn a great deal about the nature of dreaming from the general psychological point of view. From the parapsychological point of view, such techniques would show promise in leading toward laboratory production of "lucid" dreams, psychic dreams, and out-of-the-body experiences.

Several lines of evidence converge to suggest that ESP is more likely to emerge in altered states of consciousness than during normal wakefulness. On an experimental level, the occurrence of ESP in the dream phase has been confirmed in a series of studies involving electrophysiological monitoring techniques by Doctors Montague Ullman and Stanley Krippner at Maimonides Hospital in Brooklyn. Another state that has been traditionally conceptualized as an altered state of consciousness and widely associated with paranormal activity is, of course, hypnosis, the contemporary experimental literature strongly suggesting that it has a facilitative effect on psi.

An investigation reported by Charles Honorton indicates this. In "Significant Factors in Hypnotically-Induced Clairvoyant Dreams," (*Journal* A.S.P.R., January 1972) Honorton discusses an attempt to elucidate factors associated with successful ESP incorporation in hypnotic dreams, with a clarification of the role of hypnosis in their production. Honorton discovered that highly suggestible subjects in the hypnotic group assigned significantly high ratings to correct target-dream pairs. Subjects in the hypnosis group with medium or low suggestibility scores and subjects in the waking-imagination group produced chance results.

The way the tests were conducted was that target pictures, reproductions of famous paintings, were placed in opaque envelopes and laid on the arms of the hypnotized subjects' chairs. They were told to dream about the contents of the envelopes. A few examples of the kinds of results that occurred in the high suggestibility hypnosis group are:

First Dream Report: "The Virgin Mary. A statue and Jesus Christ. An old church with two pillars overgrown with grass by the church entrance. The Virgin Mary was holding Jesus as a baby."

The target picture was *The Adoration of the Shepherds* by El Greco. This painting shows the Virgin Mary holding the infant Christ. There are shepherds around them, and green leaves from a tree are visible by the opening in the structure behind the figure. The structure itself could be vaguely described as two pillars and as a church entrance.

Fourth Dream Report: "I was looking at a picture but I was in it too. I was at the beach. There were two people on a blanket. Nothing was moving. It was like a wax museum or something—people, water, etc. but nothing was moving. The water was deep blue. It was sunny. I was wearing blue too. Nothing moved, not even the water! Like everyone was frozen solid."

The target had been *Boating* by Édouard Manet. It shows a man and woman in a small sailboat. The water behind them is blue. The woman wears a blue dress; the man has a straw hat. There seems to be little animation in the picture. The figures are unmoving, almost as if frozen.

Second Dream Report from the hypnosis group of medium suggestibility: "A lot of color—blotches of it. Objects of color scooping upward. A man—I couldn't see his face. He was looking out, away from the picture. He had dark hair. Colors—blue."

The target was *Scipio the Model* by an unknown artist. It pictures a black man with his bare back facing the picture, his head resting on his arm. The figure is wearing blue trousers.

18. ESP Research Today

FOR ALL THOSE therapists who are using hypnosis with completely closed minds about any possibility that extrasensory phenomena can occur, there are other researchers using the techniques to investigate the supernormal. Hypnosis has proved an excellent tool for their needs, for, as Charles Honorton said, altered states of consciousness are favorable to the production of ESP, and hypnosis produces an altered state of consciousness.

For twenty-five years a hypnotist and past president of three societies dedicated to this art, Alwyn Stevenson accomplished some successful testing in telepathy at a distance at an army camp. As reported in "Hypnotizing by Telepathy" (*Fate*, October 1960), he discovered that hypnosis by concentration can be accomplished today just as it was in the time of Dr. Janet or Dr. Boirac. He can do it only with highly conditioned subjects, who can also be awakened by mental command. In the instances to be given the subject was *always* unaware of the presence of the operator and at no time was given any indication that he or she was going to be "thought" to sleep.

Stevenson wrote: "While stationed at Camp Halobird, just outside the city of Baltimore, I was an instructor in the Counter Intelligence Corps. In the evenings I gave demonstrations of hypnotism for the enlightenment and entertainment of the men stationed on the base. As a result of these nightly shows I had many excellent conditioned subjects."

The first incident occurred in the Post Exchange one evening while Stevenson was standing in a phone booth waiting for a long distance call-back. He saw one of his good somnambulistic subjects enter, walk over to a table with a soft drink in his hand, and sit down with his back toward the phone booth. A thought came to Stevenson's mind: "Wouldn't it be wonderful if I could put him into a hypnotic state without resorting to a written or verbal command or visual signal of any kind?" He decided to try.

Closing his eyes, facing in the general direction of the subject, Stevenson thought one word forcibly over and over again: "Sleep . . . sleep . . . sleep." He held the mental picture of the youth seated at the table and concentrated on that one word. After about half a minute he heard the sound of breaking glass. On opening his eyes, he saw to his utter amazement that the subject had slumped over the table, his glass had tipped and spilled, and the soft drink bottle lay shattered on the floor where it had fallen. Stevenson left the phone booth and hurried over to check the soldier, whom he found in deep trance. When awakened, the youth could give no explanation as to why he suddenly went to sleep, for he had had no slightest premonition that it was coming on.

An opportunity to test the authenticity of Stevenson's first experience occurred three days later. He wrote: "I was passing one of the restaurants on the field and through the front plate glass window noticed three girls seated at a table, one of them a civilian typist who was an excellent subject. I entered the restaurant through the kitchen in the rear of the building for I didn't want her to see me, and ended up in a washroom with a brick wall between us."

Once again he closed his eyes and concentrated forcibly on the word "sleep." In about thirty seconds he heard screams and excited talk in the dining room. He went in to find that his subject had gone into a hypnotic state with a burning cigarette in her fingers. As she slumped over the table, her companions thought she had fainted. When she awakened, she, too, insisted she'd had no feeling of the hypnotic state coming on.

Stevenson tried this on seven other subjects and met with complete failure. He was led to the eventual conclusion that only *certain* subjects can receive telepathic impulses.

The next time he attempted it, however, he met with double success. Passing the supply room he saw another conditioned subject seated at a desk with his back towards the door. "I made no sound, stared at the back of his head and attempted to put him to sleep by mental command," he said. "Again, success! He collapsed in his chair." When Stevenson entered the room to awaken this young man, he says that what he saw was staggering. On a pile of blankets in a far corner of the room lay another of his subjects sprawled out loosely—unmistakably also in deep hypnotic sleep. "I had not even been aware of his presence!" he writes.

On another occasion, Stevenson attempted to hypnotize a conditioned subject in a book store and instead reached a girl who worked as a soda jerk in a drug store half a block away! When he told this story to a psychologist, he received a warning that has stuck with him: "Be careful! Telepathy knows no distance!"

Lee Edwards Levinson, who also uses the pen name Lee Edwards, has written television specials, documentaries, and dramatic scripts for the three major networks as well as articles for prominent magazines. In addition he does hypnosis and ESP research. In an article entitled, "Hypnosis: The Key to Unlocking Latent Psi Faculties" for the *International Journal of Parapsychology* (1968) he made certain contentions on the basis of a series of qualitative experiments with nine subjects:

Most hypnotized somnambulists are capable of demonstrating telepathy or clairvoyance, and in some instances both. Somnambulists may be trained to exhibit their psi skills with marked consistency whether in deep trance or in the waking state. Their target hits are predictable and well above chance expectation. The faith-prestige relationship between hypnotist and subject is a major factor in facilitating psi performance.

Among Levinson's illustrations were the following:

S-1 was by far the most shy and introspective somnambulist of the group. The youth had facial acne, which was partially responsible for his withdrawn attitude, making him self-conscious. But when hypnotized his over-all performance was very high; his errors were minimal. On one occasion the operator selected six first names for transmission mentally, and the subject scored six precise and consecutive target hits. Some of the names were fairly common; others were unusual.

Distance tests were conducted. With the subject remaining

seated, the operator, accompanied by two observers, left the sitting room for another room located at the opposite end of the house. This was to alleviate the argument that there might have been unconscious whispering. After they had reached their destination, they selected five names. The operator conversed with the subject by way of an extension telephone in order to repeat the following phrases: "Are you ready? Now I am beginning to think." He then transmitted at thirty-second intervals each of the selected names. S-1, in trance with his eyes open, recorded his answers on a pad that had been left in his hands. After the final target had been projected, the three returned to the sitting room to compare the target answers. S-1 had again responded accurately with five precise target hits.

S-1 was also tested for his clairvoyant skills. On several occasions the operator retired to a nearby room while S-1 remained in trance seated by the extension telephone. Since confusion arises at times in deciding whether the phenomenon that occurs is really telepathy or clairvoyance, the operator avoided the telepathic process by selecting the current issue of *Life* magazine and, with his eyes closed, turning to a page selected at random. The magazine was placed in an outstretched position with the cover facing the operator. S-1 was then asked on the telephone to describe the page the operator had pointed to with his index finger. Afterward, it was turned over and examined. S-1 had described in detail the colors of clothing people wore, the brand name of products, and other pertinent details. At first, S-1 complained that the pages appeared "fuzzy"; he saw them as through a "mist." Encouraged with positive suggestions, S-1 gradually found his vision improving until he could perceive the magazine pages as though he were looking directly at them with his eyes open.

In the capacity of traveling clairvoyance, the entranced S-1 in one test traveled a mile away to the home of a friend of the operator's known only to him and to no one else present at the sitting. S-1 described in detail the movements and conversations of the operator's friend and his family. At the conclusion of the experiment, the facts given by S-1 were verified by telephoning the family that the boy had psychically visited.

Levinson's subject called S-4 was a thirty-two-year-old Florida housewife and mother of two, who was an excellent artist-sculptor and who owned an art gallery in Miami. Her highest hits as a receiver during telepathy experiments were in correctly describing target paintings projected to her by him and subsequently by other operators. Her high scores were motivated by her personal interest in art.

On one occasion, Levinson issued the following post-hypnotic suggestion to S-4: "Immediately upon awakening you will leave the room. When I ask you to return to where I am seated, you will reenter the room and find an object I have hidden. As soon as you locate the object, you will bring it to me." When S-4 was awakened, she left the room as instructed, accompanied by two persons. A committee of three stayed in the sitting room, the operator allowing them to select and hide an object of their choosing. First they hid a key high above a window sill, but then decided to transfer it to another hiding place. It was finally stashed in the brassiere of the only other woman present during this experiment. Then S-4 was asked to return.

Immediately on returning to the room, S-4 instinctively walked straight to the original hiding place and exclaimed aloud: "Whatever it is you've hidden, I feel it was placed here first," pointing to the window sill, "but I don't feel it's on this side of the room any longer." Asked what the object was and where it was now hidden, S-4 responded: "It's small. I feel it is metallic." The operator, upon hearing the word "metallic," mentally projected the word-picture "key." At that precise moment, S-4's lips parted with a knowing smile and she said complacently: "It's a key." Assured by her sudden insight, she walked over to the only other woman present, pointed to her bosom and said: "They've placed it inside there, but I'm not going to retrieve it."

S-2 was a fifteen-year-old New York City high school sophomore. One one occasion, the operator issued the following posthypnotic suggestion to him: "When you awaken, your cousin will no longer be in the room. He had to go home." The subject then was awakened, and Levinson placed a handkerchief in the cousin's hands. Astounded, S-2 was anxious to know how that handkerchief was floating in the air. This posthypnotic hallucination was particularly effective because the operator had instructed the subject to stand in front of the handkerchief, directly in line with his cousin, and to "see" straight across the room. The operator stood directly behind the subject's cousin, an encyclopedia in his hand, and leafed through the volume without looking at the face of the page he then selected. S-2 told the exact page turned to and the phrase Levinson's finger was pointing to at the time. This demonstration of clairvoyance in the waking state was repeated several times with the same encyclopedia during the course of this test.

In July 1958, Dr. Stanley V. Mitchell, president of the International Guild of Hypnotists, was touring Europe, conducting various experiments and demonstrations in the countries he visited. In Russia, while at the Ganushina Psychoneurological Clinic, he met Dr. Vojutsko and his assistant, two men in their forties who spoke English fairly well. They were friendly and seemed as interested in what those in the United States were doing with hypnosis as he was in their work; so they took him on a tour of the institute and explained the various types of cases with which they worked.

Mitchell's report of his experience was published in "Can Hypnosis Break Through the Language Barrier?" (*Fate*, February 1963): "I was tremendously impressed. In no other single place have I seen so much fine equipment devoted to hypnosis and allied fields." They had many complicated devices designed to facilitate hypnotic therapy—such as spinning discs with colors on them to fix the subject's attention and gradually close his eyes in hypnotic sleep.

When they asked Mitchell for a demonstration of the usual American techniques, quite different from theirs, they called in a young nurse to be the subject. The doctor explained to her, in Russian, that Mitchell was going to hypnotize her. She nodded and sat down in the chair indicated. Mitchell says: "I stood in front of her and took a deep breath, held it a few seconds and exhaled. I motioned for her to do the same, to assist her in relaxing. Snapping on my per-light I held it slightly above her head—not beaming it into her eyes—but, nevertheless, holding her gaze in focus."

"Your eyes are becoming very tired," he said in English. "Your eyelids are getting so heavy all you want to do is to close them." So she closed them and went promptly into a state of trance. When he suggested, in English, that heaviness and limpness were felt throughout her body, she responded, even to letting her head droop forward. He told her that her arm was becoming lighter and slowly rising. It rose until it was outstretched at her shoulder level. Then he suggested it would become rigid and numb, without feeling. Asking for a needle, he pricked her right hand. She showed no reaction whatever; but when he pricked her left hand she immediately withdrew it. He then suggested her right arm would become normal and drop back into her lap when he snapped his fingers. It did. Then he told her she would feel refreshed and energetic when he counted to five and would be wide awake, and she complied.

The Russian doctors seemed abnormally excited about this, and Mitchell learned why after they had held an animated discussion with the nurse. She did not know one word of English! It was then Mitchell's turn to be excited and puzzled. "Had I known the nurse didn't understand English I would never have dreamed of attempting the demonstration," he said. Had the Russian techniques of hypnosis been anything like his own, he would have suspected that she just did the normal things she believed to be expected of her. But he had already observed that the Russians used lights and whirling devices and various other systems of quite a different nature.

Another time on that trip Mitchell had a similar experience. In Warsaw a group of people interested in hypnosis visited his hotel room. When one man asked to be hypnotized, the woman sitting behind him went off into a state of trance at the same time he did. And she did not speak English! Through an interpreter, she later asked for another treatment because she was having difficulty sleeping. And eighteen months later she came to Chicago and while there contacted him to have the suggestions reenforced.

To give her as much assistance and confidence as possible I suggested she attend my weekly class in self-hypnosis on the following evening. My intention was to have our medical director,

Dr. R. S. Ziehn, who speaks German, which she also speaks, give her the suggestions while she was in a state of hypnosis.

She came to the class and was hypnotized in German, but upon awakening she told Dr. Ziehn that she had not felt the sensations he'd suggested as intensely as she had felt them when I placed her in the state of hypnosis in Warsaw, and on the previous day in Chicago. He asked how I had made these suggestions and she told him she had not understood what I had said but she had felt the physical suggestions I had given to her strongly.

As she put it to Mitchell later: "When you hypnotize me I can understand you easily; but when you don't, all you say is cha, cha, cha!"

"Opinion about the usefulness of hypnosis as a key to the hidden psychic abilities is now divided," wrote Jarl Fahler of Finland in "Does Hypnosis Increase Psychic Powers?" (*Tomorrow*, Autumn 1958). "Thus, there is a definite need to clarify this subject. With this in mind, I undertook a number of exploratory experiments which covered many phases of psychic activities as they relate to the hypnotic condition."

Many of these experiments were carried out at Fahler's home in Helsingfors, and later experiments were conducted at the Parapsychology Laboratory at Duke University. The experiments in Finland were often attended and witnessed by members of the Society for Psychical Research, of which Fahler was the president. In these experiments, done over a span of nearly ten years, he hypnotized many persons, totaling into the hundreds. For the complicated experiments only subjects able to enter the deepest, or somnambulic, stage were able to achieve noteworthy results.

One of Fahler's best subjects was a woman he refers to as "Mrs. S——" who had never previously exhibited much psychic ability. With her as a subject, he was able to carry out a series of dramatic experiments called the "water glass" tests, which were done in the presence of six to eight witnesses and were recorded by a secretary at the time they occurred. In these tests an individual's sense of touch and feeling can be connected somehow with an object outside his body.

Here is the report of one test, conducted on November 11, 1953:

Mrs. S—— was brought into deep hypnosis. Two similar glasses, both filled with the same amount of water, were placed in front of her on a table. Fahler took one glass and put it between her hands. He then gave verbal suggestions to her that all sense of feeling and pain was being drained from her arms and hands into the water glass and that the arms and hands, at the same time, were becoming insensitive to feeling.

After these suggestions had been repeated a few times, their results were tested by sticking a needle into the water in the glass. The subject reacted with a jerk of her arms and hands. The needle was then stuck into her arms and hands, but there was no reaction whatever. When the glass was removed from her hands and placed on the table, the results were the same as before when the needle was used. Even when the glass was taken into an adjoining room, her reactions were the same when a needle was pushed into the water. When the glass was outside the house, the results were identical. On one occasion while Mrs. S—— was in deep trance, one of the observers took the glass into another room, closing the door behind him. A few minutes afterward, the subject smiled and moved her arms. Fahler asked her what was happening, and she replied, "Mr. O—— is blowing warm and sometimes cool air on my arms."

When Mr. O—— returned he told them he had been blowing on the surface of the water glass. This experiment was also repeated many times with the same results.

Another series of interesting experiments Fahler conducted with Mrs. S—— might be called the game of "hunt the needle." While she was somnambulistic, a small object, such as an iron nail or a needle, would be hidden in an adjoining room. Her hands would have touched the object before it was hidden, to provide some feeling of contact. Then she was given the suggestion that, upon awakening and hearing a certain word spoken, she would immediately "be dragged" to the object that had been hidden.

As an instance of this, Mrs. S—— was told that after she was awakened when Fahler said the word "now" she would go to the place where the object had been hidden and find it without any difficulty. Then Mrs. O—— hid a small nail in a place that nobody else knew. After she returned, Fahler woke Mrs. S—— by counting to ten, and she chatted with the others until he used the word "now." She reacted to that at once by leaving her chair and going into the adjoining room and from there into the entrance hall. There she stood for a while, and then stretched her hand toward a pile of hats on a shelf. She took the nail, which had been hidden in Mrs. O——'s furry hat, returned to the experiment room and showed it to everyone.

Dr. John Björkhem, the Swedish psychotherapist mentioned earlier, has conducted numerous experiments with students of Upsala University. During one of his traveling clairvoyance experiments with a young Lapp girl of exceptional ability, he asked her, while under deep hypnosis, to visit her home several hundred miles away and tell him what her parents were doing. She described in detail the movements of her parents and even recited the precise paragraph from a newspaper her father was reading.

An interesting sequel to this occurred shortly after the test. Her parents telephoned, frightened because her apparition had just appeared to them!

19. ESP Conditioning

Much of today's ESP research is done in laboratories under conditions as controlled as those of any other scientific discipline. With Dr. Pagenstecher of Mexico City as a forerunner, and Dr. Milan Ryzl, formerly of Prague and now of California, as today's prime exponent, it is being learned how to train subjects under hypnosis to have ESP ability.

Ryzl, who in his native country worked as a physicist and chemist with the Institute of Biology, Czechoslovakian Academy of Science, has been a parapsychologist for nearly twenty years. While still in Europe he devised a technique for training hypnotic subjects to improve their psi faculties, and he believes his method may make it possible to a greater or lesser degree to train extrasensory abilities in all people. He has several sensationally successful subjects who testify to the truth of his premise.

Ryzl settled in the United States in 1967, when he joined the staff of Dr. J. B. Rhine's Institute of Parapsychology. He

later moved to San José, California. He is the author of
Parapsychology: A Scientific Approach (New York, 1970).

Sheila Ostrander and Lynn Schroeder describe Ryzl in
their book *Psychic Discoveries Behind the Iron Curtain*:

With a quick eye and a quick comment for what's going on about
him, the forty-one-year-old Ryzl is a man of many personalities.
There is the electric, freewheeling Ryzl—even his hair, full and
wavy, has an electric, half-tamed look—who'll take a chance and
bet on a horse one of his psychics sees winning a race. This is the
one-step-ahead-of-the-pack Ryzl, who managed to get out of
Czechoslovakia in late 1967 during the hardline Novotny regime,
bringing with him to America not just a hastily packed suitcase,
but also his wife, his two sons, his assistant, his library, and his
car.

But there is also Ryzl the careful, methodical scientist who
has produced some fine contemporary ESP work. While he
was still in Prague he became a research associate of the
Parapsychology Laboratory at Duke and the only Communist
ever to receive the McDougall Award, which was given by
the Parapsychology Association for distinguished work in the
field.

Ryzl is particularly good at encouraging others to learn to
use their psychic powers. He says, "I believe most people
have latent psychic ability. The problem today is to devise
methods of evoking this talent and bringing it under conscious control."

To use his techniques, the first thing you must find is a
subject willing to spend much time and effort in order to
learn to acquire such an unusual ability as psi. Then you
have to work with him and keep him busy for a long while.
Some people learn faster than others, of course.

Ability of the subject to hallucinate freely under direction is a major indication that he will probably be successful. Ryzl believes in verbal encouragement, assuring the subject of his success, telling him he can and must develop his psychic ability. Then simple tests are given in which the subject may demonstrate elementary clairvoyant ability. With a good subject this is not difficult to achieve.

The second phase of the experiment consists of a long and intense training period. It is now that the subject is encouraged to use his ESP faculties consciously.

In referring to artificially induced hallucinations with hypnotized subjects, Ryzl reports in "A Method of Training in ESP" (*International Journal of Parapsychology*, 1966):

The subject is now living subjectively in a state of insulation from the world outside, "forgetful" of anything beyond his interrelationship with the experimenter. His attention is focused on the experimenter's words: his normally spontaneous mental processes have been quieted and inhibited; his sensory perceptions are limited to his rapport with the hypnotist. We might describe this state, somewhat paradoxically, as a state of active mental inactivity, in which the subject's unconsciousness is closed to incoming stimuli from the somatic senses and becomes susceptible to stimuli of an extrasensory nature. We endeavor to enhance the subject's suggestibility as much as possible by giving him increasingly more and more complicated suggestions, and by making him accept them.

Lee Edwards Levinson amplifies this thought somewhat: "Ryzl's theory might be furthered to include the hypothesis that the very nature of the intensely personalized interrelationship between the hypnotist and the subject allows for the spontaneous creation of a state of 'oneness.' The participants are so deeply attuned to each other that this state in effect acts as a catalyst eliciting paranormal phenomena."

In the next phase of the experiment the subject is taught to achieve for himself the state of consciousness in which he is receptive to ESP. He can then use his ESP faculties consciously.

In the *Journal* of the Society for Psychical Research (March 1962) Ryzl goes further into his method of training, which, he says, is an exacting, tiring process that requires much patience on the part of the experimenter and of the subject. He originally started his training program with more than five hundred subjects, university student volunteers between the ages of sixteen and thirty. It took diligence on their part, but more than 10 percent of them managed to achieve some success and were eventually able to accomplish simple ESP demonstrations without outside assistance.

Two of Ryzl's subjects have been outstanding: Pavel Stepanek and a young woman he designates as Miss J.K. A typical ESP experiment with the hypnotized Miss J.K. involved ESP cards wrapped in several layers of stiff opaque paper and put into heavy envelopes so opaque they excluded entirely the possibility of cognizing by normal means. These were placed into her hands. The experimenter did not know which symbols were in which envelopes, and the subject and the envelopes were always in his sight. Checking was performed after the completion of each series of trials. In clairvoyantly calling out which cards were in which envelopes, out of 250 calls the subject achieved 121 hits. Chance expectancy was 50 hits.

In a control series, without hypnosis and with no ESP expectations, under the same conditions, 250 calls yielded 46 hits.

Miss J.K., Ryzl's favorite subject until Stepanek came along, was twenty-one years old and from a family half

Czech and half German. By his fourth experiment with her he began to have good results, and she began to learn to have conscious control of her ESP ability so she could use it under varying conditions. As the subject became more used to hypnosis the time required for psi attainment became shorter and shorter. At this phase of her training there were several instances when ESP appeared spontaneously while she was in the waking state and absorbed in thought.

Later, Dr. Ryzl says: "J.K. began to make practical use of her ability in various situations of her daily life." When she lost the keys to her flat, Ryzl made her ascertain clairvoyantly where they were. Another time she and her hypnotist were in a strange country town and wished to go to the cinema, but she had forgotten the way. He hypnotized her, and she saw the way, and they went there with no trouble.

It was not until about nine months after Miss J.K. began her training that she reached the stage where she could apply her ESP ability at will without depending on Ryzl. Once when several important documents of hers had been mislaid and lost at her work, she independently used her clairvoyant powers and found the documents hidden away in a place hitherto unknown to her.

Ryzl sums up his discussion of Miss J.K. by stating that present research has shown that by means of hypnosis it is possible to train the ESP ability to such an extent that it is governable by will and applicable as an additional sense that, in cooperation with the other senses, enables us to orientate ourselves in the outer world.

In one year's training, Miss J.K.'s ESP ability was developed to such a degree that although she is not able to apply it on every occasion, yet it appears in all cases when suitable inner psychological conditions prevail.

Another subject, known as Miss S.K., produced certain instances of visualization that clarify for us something about the technique she used. A pair of steel scissors with a dim luster had been placed somewhat opened behind an opaque screen in front of her. She followed the usual gradual process in visualizing them. She first saw the object indistinctly, blurred, as if in a fog, and the operator told her that the picture must gradually get more distinct. She reported her impressions as follows: "First a series of quickly changing pictures appeared; such notions were dancing before my eyes as if a quickened film were being projected." Then she described a metallic color with dim luster, an acute angle, an obtuse angle. Then the acute angle became more distinct to her vision. She noticed there were two acute angles with their tips pointing toward each other. "It reminds me of two crossed pencils . . . it is decidedly not pencils . . . the ends away from me are pointed . . . but those near to me do not want to appear to me. I have not got it sharp enough. It strikes me as if two circles were projecting out of a thick fog . . . it's a pair of scissors."

Sometimes the subjects begin to have inhibitions about the growth of their ESP. Because a psychic or sensitive or medium is considered "different" by society, a talented subject may become afraid he is developing something undesirable; he may fear an invasion of his private life or ridicule from his fellows.

One who has never seemed to go through this phase is Pavel Stepanek, Ryzl's most famous psychic student. He has never refused to put his gift at the disposal of science, sometimes even taking vacation days from his job to do it. To hear grateful scientists tell it, the most amazing thing about Stepanek, a bachelor in his late thirties, is his modest, cheerful, ever cooperative personality. Unlike everyone else, he seems to get an actual kick out of card tests.

When he first came to Ryzl he demonstrated no extrasensory abilities. But his usual tenacity and persistence made it possible for the parapsychologist to study his performance over a period of three years as his ESP developed. His successes were not dramatic, but his consistent performance, in Ryzl's opinion, proves that the two greatest handicaps in ESP testing—the difficulty in developing latent extrasensory abilities to the point of conscious application and its unreliability —can be overcome.

After he had developed under hypnosis, Stepanek was usually given a standard ESP test, and he could perform for visiting parapsychologists as well as for his own operator. The test Pavel uses almost exclusively consists of two-color cards, 5×3 inches, that are hidden from view in opaque envelopes. At first the cards were black on one side and white on the other, but now the black side has been changed to green. It is always a matter of selecting out of two possibilities where the probable total of chance hits is 50 percent, for all Stepanek has to do is to know which card is uppermost.

Ryzl's tests of Stepanek were rigidly controlled. The hypnotized subject was to name the face-up color of cards in a series of ten two-color cards enclosed in opaque envelopes. The sets of ten cards were chosen in random order by an assistant who then handed them to the Czechoslovakian parapsychologist. There was no conversation. Ryzl sat in the center of the room facing the subject but separated from him by an opaque screen. He cut the pack of cards, then laid them, still in their envelopes, on the table before him. It was the subject's task to name correctly the up-color of each card. To guard against error the calls were recorded independently by both Ryzl and his assistant. At the conclusion of a run, each experimenter independently compared the contents of the envelopes with the subject's recorded calls. Finally the two compared their own findings, then the assistant took the cards out of their envelopes and checked Stepanek's accuracy. Under these stringent conditions two hundred sets were run, a total of two thousand individual cards. Stepanek scored 1,144 hits and 856 misses, a number significantly above chance expectancy.

In January and February 1963, Dr. J. Gaither Pratt of the University of Virginia visited Prague, where he joined Ryzl in conducting similar experiments. Pratt prepared the cards in the adjoining room, and Ryzl submitted them to the subject as before. Both men kept a record of Stepanek's calls. At the conclusion of the test Pratt compared his records with the cards in the envelopes and found Pavel had scored 1,133 hits out of a possible 2,000.

The Czech scientist's prize subject has gone on to higher glories, although still sticking to his green and white cards. As Sheila Ostrander and Lynn Schroeder say of him: "Stepanek seemed to be a man for the long haul. He's kept right on racking up impressive scores on the tests. Yet, as a psychic, he's a sort of Johnny-one-note."

"It's a curious thing," Ryzl comments, "Stepanek's clairvoyance always moved in that one channel, etching it deeper and deeper. Apparently this single ability to score well on the tests satisfied whatever motivation or need he has for a sixth sense."

Pavel's sticking to his one and only test has not hurt his career, however. Pratt is enchanted with him. Approximately twenty original research reports on work done with him have already been published, for the total number of trials he has made in well-controlled ESP tests is the largest on record.

Pratt discovered that Pavel seemed somehow to relate clairvoyantly to favored cards, seemingly to know when favorites are presented no matter how well they are wrapped. Pratt is wholeheartedly on the trail of this "focusing effect," having even discovered that Pavel not only has favorite cards, but that he also began to focus on certain envelopes that held these cards, even though there were no visual or physical clues, no differences at all. These envelopes were then put inside covers. Still Pavel could focus on his favorites. Eventually, some of the covers also showed focusing, and these were then fitted into jackets. In recent tests, Pavel has been presented with packages containing card, envelope, cover, and jacket, one inside the other, and still he achieves greater than chance expectancy.

All this is a little bit complicated for the lay reader to comprehend, so let us leave it to the scientists and be glad they are working at it. It helps to better the reputation of the harlot hypnosis; by letting her into the laboratory her status is bound to improve.

Dr. Harold A. Cahn, who is conducting tests of a similar nature—using hypnosis to develop ESP in his subjects—at the College of Scientific and Humanistic Studies at Northern Arizona University, Flagstaff, says in "My Approach to Parapsychology—a 'White Paper',": "By approaching psi phenomena scientifically, granting even that this may lead to a conceptual revision of science itself, one can distinguish between the solidly grounded and the speculative. For this operational reason plus the advantages conferred by laboratory methodology, the scientific approach may be pedestrian but in many ways safer than through emotionalism or pure speculation."

Ryzl, glad that his success with the cultivation of ESP and its volitional control has rendered the faculty substantially less elusive than hitherto believed, is delighted that he has helped to bring ESP to the stage where it can, as a relatively constant ability, be subjected to laboratory investigations. He has even higher hopes for it, however. When he arrived in America, the Bulletin of Dr. Rhine's Foundation for Research on the Nature of Man quoted Ryzl:

The developments in the natural sciences, and, of course, the whole trend of the development of modern civilization have given emphasis to the material and technical aspects of life. In today's civilization man is drawn more and more away from his inner life. In my opinion, parapsychological research could reverse this trend and direct man's attention also to other aspects of his cosmic existence and to other forces and components of his personality.

20. ESP in Russia

RUSSIA IS WAY AHEAD of America in some aspects of ESP research. In other aspects we are ahead of them, even though they have been actively engaged in it for a good while. Hypnotic telepathic experiments have been going on there since as early as 1923, the I. V. Pavlov Institute in Moscow having, for many years, done a great deal of original research. Quite naturally, the Pavlovian approach, emphasizing utilization of conditioned reflexes, has been basic to the Institute's policy.

The late Professor Leonid Vasiliev, Director of Leningrad University's Physiology Department, studied hypnotelepathic phenomena for more than forty years. He proved conclusively that previously conditioned subjects may be hypnotized telepathically from a distance without the aid of posthypnotic suggestion.

From Martin Ebon's book *Psychic Discoveries by the Russians* we learn that "Vasiliev had joined the Brain Research Institute in 1921. The following year he became a member of its Committee for the Study of Mental Suggestion, which specialized in studying the 'effect of mental suggestion on a hypnotized human subject.' The term 'mental suggestion', as then used, was equivalent to telepathy as it is now used. Its findings were submitted to the Second All-Russian Congress of Psychoneurology in 1924. The Congress encouraged Russian researchers to cooperate with the International Committee for Psychical Research. Vasiliev, throughout his life, remained in contact with the Institut Metapsychique International in Paris, of which he was a member." He was well-grounded in the early French experiments with psychic phenomena and hypnosis.

Ebon continues:

In 1928, the Brain Research Institute undertook a study of possible physical factors in telepathy with human subjects, which lasted for more than five years and led to the conclusion that phenomena of thought transference did not have an "electromagnetic" basis; this concept is now generally accepted by parapsychologists throughout the world. Vasiliev resumed his experiments after a gap of several years, reestablished contact with his Paris colleagues in 1956, and three years later published a booklet on *Mysterious Phenomena of the Human Psyche*; it appeared in Moscow, issued by the Publishing House of Political Literature in at least three successive printings and was translated into English (New Hyde Park, New York, 1965). The booklet expanded Vasiliev's 1926 paper, stating that parapsychological research could have a strictly materialistic basis and serve to counteract superstitious interpretation. He confronted the question of whether research in telepathy might be "detrimental to our materialistic viewpoint, or to the generally recognized science of physiology." He replied, "Certainly not! On the contrary, we find here a new inquiry for scientific physiology. Thus a strong and sharp weapon has been placed in the hands of materialistic-analytical science, capable of combating certain difficult-to-eradicate mystical views and assumptions."

After Vasiliev's death in 1966, emphasis on parapsychological studies in the Soviet Union temporarily shifted from Leningrad to Moscow, where conferences in this field have since been held.

Current Russian research can be traced to nineteenth-century experiments in hypnosis in which the key questions were: "Can a hypnotist influence his subject by other than verbal or standard physical signals? If so, is it possible to discover how this influence is conveyed from hypnotist to subject? Does a form of electromagnetic radiation convey the instructions? Does some disturbance of an electrical field communicate this influence? Or is the compelling message, if any, carried in some manner as yet wholly inexplicable in terms of current physical concepts?" Perhaps Dr. Boirac could have helped them.

Vasiliev began by attempting to get a hypnotic subject to move an arm, a leg, or a specific muscle without giving any verbal instructions. As their first subject, he and his associates chose a chronic patient, identified only as Kouzima, in one of Leningrad's mental hospitals. She was suffering from a long-standing hysterical paralysis of her left side. During hypnosis, they found that she could be persuaded to move her left side in response to verbal commands. What about the mental ones? Dr. V. N. Finne, an associate, placed Kouzima in a hypnotic trance through verbal suggestion. He next wrote down on a piece of paper the movements he planned to "will" her to perform. He then proceeded to imagine, as vividly as possible, the subject actually making the series of muscular contractions necessary to execute the movement, and to influence her to comply with his mental commands. All present sought to avoid unconscious whispering, which, of course, would have ruined the experiment.

The researchers found that once the subject was in a state of deep hypnosis, her eyes tightly closed or bandaged, she usually made the movement suggested to her and no others. When she was asked why she had done this, she replied: "I was told to by Dr. Finne." Among the movements suggested in this way were raising a hand or leg, putting out her tongue, crossing her arms, sitting up, putting her hands under her head, or scratching her nose. Kouzima was even suggestible by visiting scientists as well.

In 1932 Vasiliev found three highly susceptible subjects who could be hypnotized at a distance by telepathic signals, he and two of his colleagues being able to entrance them by merely wishing them to be hypnotized. Using this technique, long distance experiments were successfully performed between Leningrad and Sebastopol, over a thousand miles apart.

Vasiliev did other experiments, trying to discover the nature of telepathy, and he was able to provide a strong argument against the electromagnetic hypothesis for ESP. The hypnotist was shut up in a cabinet made of thick lead slabs (a type of Faraday cage), which screened off electromagnetic waves in a broad range of wavelengths. He was still able, telepathically, to put his subjects under hypnosis, just as before. On the basis of these experiments, Vasiliev concluded that telepathy is based on some new, hitherto unknown, energy.

Today's Soviet researchers have added physiological monitoring. Electroencephalographs attached to a hypnotic and distant subject record the moment a telepathic command is sent, and the moment the subject begins to cede consciousness.

The story of Wolf Messing, a stage telepathist and a sensitive with an outstanding gift for mind reading as well as amazing hypnotic powers, has become legendary in the Soviet Union and elsewhere in Eastern Europe. He says he was born in 1899 in Gora Kalvaria, a small, then predominantly Jewish, town near Warsaw, which was a traditional rabbinical center and residence of many famous wise men. At the age of ten he was placed in a religious school to be educated as a rabbi, but, feeling no vocation for this career and afraid to oppose his father openly, he ran away from home and finally landed in Berlin. There he found the Jewish quarter and was soon working as a messenger boy, but making very little money. One day from sheer exhaustion and starvation, he fell unconscious in the street. Taken to a hospital, he was declared dead and sent to the morgue. He would soon have been dispatched to a pauper's grave, except for the happy coincidence that a medical student detected a faint heartbeat in his apparently lifeless body. Back in the hospital, Messing attracted the attention of psychiatrist and neuropathologist Professor Abel, who took him under his care for further investigation. He discovered that the boy had paranormal possibilities, inspired him with self-confidence, and found him an impresario who henceforth took charge of the boy's future, launching him on a successful career as a stage performer.

Eventually Wolf Messing was appearing in the famous Berlin Wintergarten. In his first number he amazed the public as a fakir totally insensitive to pain, due to his ability to produce a high degree of anesthesia in various parts of his body. In his second act, he was a "miracle-detective": valuables were distributed and hidden among the audience, and Messing invariably found every single piece in record time.

The talented boy was jealously guarded from the outside world by his manager, who wanted to keep him in total dependence; but feeling an insatiable need for learning, Wolf took private lessons from tutors and read voraciously.

When the First World War broke out he was fifteen, and his manager took him to Vienna. Then during the next ten years he went on a series of world tours: from Japan to Brazil to Argentina to Australia, and the next ten years he spent in Poland. There he achieved wide success as a clairvoyant, hypnotist, mind reader, and a man with generally unusual paranormal gifts.

In 1939, when Hitler's army invaded Poland, Messing moved to Soviet Russia, where he found security, prosperity, and general esteem. He even gave his "psychological experiments" on command for Stalin. In his autobiography Messing narrates in detail two of the experiments, which, he says, were thoroughly investigated by Stalin's order.

The first test was to obtain from a cashier in the Russian State Bank 100,000 rubles in return for a blank check. Messing approached the cashier, gave him the blank check, and put his opened attaché case on the counter. The cashier glanced at the check, took 100,000 rubles from the safe, and handed them to Messing, who stuffed them into the case and joined two official witnesses in charge of the experiment. After they had duly attested that the experiment had been satisfactorily performed, Messing went back to the cashier and began handing him, one after the other, the sealed packages of banknotes. The cashier looked at him, looked at the blank check on his desk, and dropped in a dead faint on the floor. Luckily, adds Messing, the shock was not fatal.

The second experiment consisted in getting out without a pass from the office of a high official, who was protected by three sets of guards—each of which was instructed not to let Messing out. With his ability to hypnotize people, he had no trouble leaving; but, Messing said: "Once in the street I glanced up at the window of the room I had just left, and seeing the official standing there. I couldn't help myself, and waved my hand to him."

In his memoirs Messing quotes the above case with the following comment: "This and similar facts should make us reconsider the often advanced opinion that nobody would perform under hypnosis an act opposed to his convictions. I have no doubt that the guards would not let me pass if I had directed at them the suggestion to let me pass as myself; but, using my mental power, I made them see in me the high official whom they would let out without a pass. Likewise a man under hypnosis can be told to shoot at a rabbit when in fact he would be shooting at a man."

It is hardly wise to accept what a man puts into his autobiography as unassailable fact; but we can at least acknowledge that here is another sound argument for the dangers of hypnosis.

Tofik Dadashev the Telepath was born in Baku, Azerbaijan, in 1947. As a child he was sensitive, imaginative, and extremely absent-minded. He was fourteen or fifteen when he first experimented with his telepathic and hypnotic powers. During a boring literature class in school he idly wondered if, by mental concentration, he could make the teacher stutter. After he had been concentrating for a few minutes the teacher became visibly nervous and began to stutter and read like a first-form pupil.

This demonstration of his mental power over people excited Tofik, and he tried it on other teachers. Soon he had them walking aimlessly up and down the aisles, approaching his desk, and then turning back. To make up for this disruption, he also helped to subdue rowdy classmates, calming them down by silent suggestion.

For some time Tofik concealed these special abilities from his family. When he was eighteen, living with relatives in Kiev and studying in a technical school, he saw one of Wolf Messing's performances on stage and realized that he possessed the same miraculous abilities. Now he took his relatives into his confidence, and they readily agreed to cooperate with simple tasks to test him, such as hiding a coin and having Tofik find it by reading their minds. He also used them as subjects in his first attempts at hypnotism. A year later, having acquired confidence in his ability, he set off for Moscow to demonstrate his talents before experts with the aim of becoming a performer like Messing. He was given intricate tests in order to prove that he could read minds. One was to enter a large room containing many different articles and pick out the one his examiners were thinking of. Another was to select the right book in a library, open it at the right page, and find the right word or sentence. It is reported that Tofik passed these tests brilliantly, without making any errors.

A rather weird technique used by Dr. Vladimir L. Raikov is described by Ostrander and Schroeder. It is what he calls "artificial reincarnation." A visitor to an art studio with Raikov was told: "I want you to meet one of my best students." A young girl in her early twenties stood up, rather grudgingly it seemed, but then she came up to the visitor and extended her hand. "I am Raphael of Urbino," she said.

Yes, she had been hypnotized into believing she was the great painter Raphael, and her drawing had improved gradually under that belief.

Ostrander and Schroeder say:

> This reincarnation of Raphael in Ira, a young science student, has not sent psychiatrist Raikov on a hunt through cobwebs and crumbling churchyards records to corroborate the girl's tale of a glorious past life. Raikov, who works with the Popov parapsychologists, knows how this Raphael became reincarnated—just as he knows how the other three Raphaels in the class came into the flesh again. Raikov called them into being. He is a master hypnotist.

With this unusual technique, Raikov is trying to evoke the birth of talent, and even genius, in his students. He believes that few people, if any, realize the extraordinary powers they possess. Not surprisingly, when back to normal the students at first refuse to believe they've drawn the pictures shown them. They probably don't even want to believe they've forged "Raphael" or the name of any other famous painter to the pictures. As the sessions progress, however, the drawing skills they acquire under hypnosis begin to become part of their own personal talents, and they become aware that they can draw well after all. By the tenth session their new talent has stabilized and become part of their conscious equipment, and it stays with them after that. Dr. Raikov thinks his type of reincarnation gives the students the opportunity of using some part of the 90 percent of their brain cells that usually lie dormant.

Psychic Discoveries Behind the Iron Curtain says that since the turn of the century Russians have honed their hypnotic skill and widely explored its possibilities. "In the

Soviet Union hypnotism is a common tool like x-rays, used in medicine, psychotherapy, physiology, psychology, and experimental pedagogy."

With the help of hypnosis, Russian scientists are researching the abilities of the mind. They have, for instance, found that in hypnotic trance a person can tell exactly how many trees and telephone poles he passed on his route from home to the doctor's office. One wonders, of course, who did the verifying count to make sure his tally was correct.

21. Clever Hands

I AM SAVING my favorite hypnosis story for last. I came across it when asked by my friends Peggy and Merl Williams of Warner Springs, California, to help them edit a manuscript about their experiences. *Hands Across Space* by Lee Gladden and Peggy Williams is the result of their endeavors, and it goes in detail into the many fantastic, curious, and delightful episodes that evolved from their study of what appears to have been a charming outer space creature contacted when a young girl was hypnotized. In no other case have I seen so many records, tapes, and volumes of transcriptions as have been acquired here during the seven year study of the hypnotic subject and the amazing entity she produced when in trance. There was no record these people did not retain, no stone they left unturned in order to achieve a complete and thorough account of every detail of the case, which was subject to objective scrutiny at all times. The results are, quite naturally, completely problematical—but what an enchanting problem!

Lee Gladden, psychology and philosophy professor at Riverside City College, Riverside, California, and a skillful hypnotist, acquired this problem when he first gave a demonstration of suggestibility to one of his classes, and one girl proved to be particularly apt. To protect the anonymity of this young lady, they call her Robin Greenwood. She is now married to a successful professional man, and she is active in social service work, so she is afraid the use of her real name will prejudice their careers. But she is a pleasant, intelligent young mother of two beautiful little girls, definitely of critical bent, well-educated, and I am sure completely unable to resort to conscious subterfuge.

What her subconscious may have done is quite another thing—and she, Lee Gladden, Peggy and Merl Williams, and others who carried on the investigation have all given credence to the possibility that the adorable monster may have been an invention of her own unconscious mind. But what if he wasn't? We're allowed to consider that possibility too.

Slender and exotic, of foreign birth but raised in the United States, Robin Greenwood was just a young college student when Lee first met her and tested her. Because of her high susceptibility to suggestion, he invited her to be the subject at a Reality Research Workshop he conducted fortnightly on Thursday evenings. It was on the night of April 24, 1957 that he first attempted age regression with her and took her back to her childhood by suggestion. After she spoke at the age of six, he regressed her to the age of three, and then to the prenatal state, when she curled up in the fetal position in Lee's big green reclining chair. He put her into deeper trance yet, telling her: "You are going back—and back until you become a person and know who you are and can tell us about it."

Then he asked: "Do you know where you are? Is it light or
is it dark?"

The answer came in a whisper: "It's light."

"It's light?" Lee repeated.

"No, it's white."

"Where are you?"

"I don't know."

What was it he was speaking to, Lee wondered. "Are you
a person?" he asked.

Answer: I'm a person with hands.

Question: Do you have anything besides hands?

A: No, just hands.

Q: No feet? No head?

A: Nothing but hands. That's all of me—hands.

Q: How many hands?

A: Eight!

Oddly enough, even though he returned and spoke to Lee
at the next workshop session, no one in the group had the
least interest in this entity whom they began to call Hands
(what else!). It was decided that past life age regression with
Robin was not fruitful, and efforts were dropped.

The case lay static until the next winter when the Williams, who came to Lee Gladden to take a course in hypnosis, were invited to hear the original tapes of Hands' conversations. They were immediately intrigued by the many
handed entity and eager to know more about him—so interested, in fact, that they decided to finance a special project to
investigate the whole confounding mystery of him. Hands,
just as eager to communicate as they were to hear him, par-
ticipated gladly in the research. From then on, for the next
seven years, every time Robin was in trance and age re-

gressed, he was there, willing to talk and answer the many questions they asked.

Hands was revealed in time to be a lovable and childlike, but huge, being with a dome-shaped body and eight hands, with an intelligence that was perhaps somewhere between that of a human and a dog. He obviously lived on another planet, which he described as composed only of mountains, with ice and snow in the winter and heat and trees and green plants in the summer, and his home was a hole in the ground. He apparently had no sex; and, poor baby, no knowledge of any kind about sexual experiences, having arrived from the sea by a process probably metamorphic. There were many others just like Hands on the planet where he lived. They had no eyes, noses, or mouths, and acquired their food by sitting on it and absorbing it through slits on their undersides.

All communication between the hands species was by telepathy, and they spent their time just sitting around on their food eating and thinking. Everyone concentrated on kind thoughts, never those of hatred or violence. Hands, who was brighter than his fellow creatures and definitely their leader, was the only one there so enterprising as to think beyond his own life experiences and his mundane physical needs. He was, you might say, the Jonathan Livingston Seagull of the Hands community. When the Cenos people from another planet came to his, he learned from them that he could communicate with them telepathically even after they had left his place and gone back to their own. So from then on, he kept his "mental antenna" turned away from his own world in an effort to communicate with—he knew not whom or what.

As Hands described it: "I was always thinking—at the very, very beginning. And finally I thought and somebody thought back." That was Lee and Robin and the workshop group. And once the contact had been established, he was able any time the subject was hypnotized and receptive to him mentally to "come in on the beam," as it were. Apparently he could use Robin's mind in order to communicate—he giving her the thoughts telepathically and her subconscious mind in some manner translating them into English. This was a similar situation to that of the previously described past-life people who could talk in our language, even though they were not supposed to be from an era in time in which it was spoken.

There was much that was intriguing about Hands. An episode as ponderously ludicrous as Walt Disney's *Fantasia* elephants dancing in pink tutus occurred when Lee attempted to give him an intelligence test. The hypnotist also hoped it might somehow be possible to produce evidence of information that could not be contained within Robin's young brain. Since Hands apparently was not able to bring data that could not be attributed to her imagination, perhaps he could be given certain random items of information she would not be likely to be able to remember. If Lee could, for instance, assemble numerous groups of numbers and then at a later date have Hands repeat them correctly, this might at least be helpful. But the creature had to handle figures in order for this to be successful. Hands had very quickly learned to count. But it would take the solving of problems to be of any real value to Lee. Hands solved that problem speedily by employing his fellow hands people as digits. Thus, if asked the result of subtracting twenty-seven from forty-three, he simply lined up forty-three of his fellows and then requested twenty-seven to remove themselves as he counted the remainder. The childlike enthusiasm of these behemoths as they bounced around on their hands performing mathematical problems is a vision I like to hold in mind—perhaps it could be used for putting oneself to sleep nights instead of counting sheep.

As the interrogations of this intriguing entity continued, hints of a civilization far in advance of our own began to take shape when Hands described the Cenos people who had visited his planet once or twice and constructed a tremendous building there to use as a technical and research laboratory. Eventually Lee and the Williams were put in touch with these outer space men and learned a great deal about their highly developed civilization.

In the course of their communications they revealed that they had visited our world in remote ages past and attempted to help various of our civilizations. They cite, specifically, calendrical devices such as those at Nazcs, Peru, and several of the pieces of monumental architecture at Chichen-Itza, Yucatan, and in Ecuador and other countries, whose mode of construction has puzzled modern architects and engineers. They also stated that they were not interested in helping us further because man on earth has invariably and consistently fought wars, and they'd had enough of such foolishness. They washed their hands of such warlike people; and it did not seem possible to convince them that we are changing all that. Well, we are, aren't we? Even if we have nothing to show for it yet?

Of course, the fascination of this is that it was coming through the mouth of a hypnotized girl who had no prior knowledge of archeology, astronomy, or anything concerning outer space. Robin had done almost no reading outside her own specific courses in college, for she is not a person who likes to read as a pastime. And her thoughts have not ever run on the occult, the mystical, or science fiction. Yet through her the Cenos people pinpointed many areas of the world in which there are definite ruins of past civilizations that indicate achievements of construction that nobody has ever been able to explain!

A favorite topic of speculation among writers and readers of science fiction has been the question of what a civilization a million years in advance of ours would be like. If this material is what it purports to be, an interesting answer is revealed. And even if it is not, the picture of Hands and his buddies gallumping around on Planet X doing math problems will always entice.

No matter what the objectivity of the participants in this research, or of those of us who read about it (and we have to be as critical of this account as we have been of all the others discussed in this book) I still somehow like to think that maybe—just maybe—out there in the vast reaches of space there may really be a lumbering, many handed creature named Hands lying there eating and thinking—and waiting for someone to think back.

22. Respectability?

WE HAVE COME a long way and spanned a great many years as we have observed this strange human capacity known as hypnosis. Has understanding more about it helped bring it permanent respectability in our thoughts, or is it still to be compared with Dr. Lindner's woman of the streets? Since the Parapsychology Association is now affiliated with the American Association for the Advancement of Science, since there is an Academy of Parapsychology and Medicine and various other indications that ESP research is becoming scientifically acceptable, maybe the parapsychologists can drag hypnotic ESP research in on its coattails. Or, in reverse, since the A.M.A. has cautiously recognized hypnosis as a valuable medical aid, and the American Psychiatric Association has reluctantly followed suit, maybe hypnosis will pull ESP into acceptability by its apron strings. Parapsychology has a fantastic amount to offer the world, when the time comes that it is taken seriously. So does hypnosis, as we have seen.

We are today beginning to realize the potential of the human mind, even though we have not yet learned a great deal about how to reach and use its great capacities. Hypnosis may be one of the answers here. Hopefully the Russians will not learn before we do how to hypnotize themselves into fantastic memory retention, useful telepathic communication with their explorers of outer space, and all the other amazing feats that may be accomplished in the future by the proper use of this strange force.

Self-hypnosis or autosuggestion will be a very useful tool when we begin to realize its potentialities. Even to be able to use it to stop bad habits like smoking and fingernail biting is a tremendous asset to our lives. It can also be carried to much greater extremes, as was discovered by a professional violinist who applied self-hypnosis to her own work. She said that she put herself into a trance and then practiced several different ways. She might visualize the music before her and then play over and over (in hallucination only, not actually with her fingers on the strings) the difficult spots until she got them. This helped her finger memory. She also did passage practice, picking hard passages and playing them in several ways to facilitate speed and accuracy. Then she would go through the whole composition for continuity. This seemed to give her an immediate grasp of the composition as a whole. And thus she was able to practice her pieces over and over in very brief *world time* periods. It not only improved her memory strikingly but also her technical performance. Her husband, also a musician, attested to the accuracy of her statement.

Perhaps self-hypnosis may only be a way of making up our minds to accomplish something and then doing it, as Richard F. Johnson said in his *Science Digest* article. He believes we can accomplish such things with our minds by strength of determination and without hypnosis. Maybe it is all there for us to use by just learning the proper mental attitudes. The stage hypnotist tells the young man from the audience that when he snaps his fingers his whole body will become stiff and rigid as a wooden plank. The fingers snap, the man goes rigid and, sure enough, he *can* be suspended between two chairs. The audience gasps its inevitable gasp, and once again the power of hypnosis is proved. Or is it? Says Johnson:

> Although the hypnotist can lead his subject to perform impressive feats like withstanding severe pain, lifting very heavy weights and becoming a "human plank" like the young man from the audience, any normal individual who is highly motivated can do the same thing.
>
> Furthermore, it now appears misleading to say that the hypnotist's subjects behave in unusual ways because they are in a "trance." Hypnotic behavior can be more easily explained as due to a change in the subject's attitudes, expectancies and the willingness to cooperate.

Johnson concluded his article: "Within the scientific world, the main effect of this recent research has been a new interpretation of hypnosis. Hypnotism is now viewed as neither special nor mysterious. Man does not need the help of mythical forces in order to display unusual abilities such as great strength or high resistance to pain. His potential is simply much greater than he has allowed himself to believe."

While it is undoubtedly true, this statement may be a bit broad. We know there is more to the mind potential than we have allowed ourselves to believe, but let us not kick hypnosis out the window just because we presently have a new concept about it. Let us be calm and rational and consider all sides of the question.

Certainly to use an actual hypnotist in order to promote in us ideas of self-help and learning abilities might be rather far to go, even if it is true, as Lee Edwards Levinson says: "The somnambulist is in a far better position to distinguish between correct and erroneous impressions, to rely on those impressions which are correct, to analyze errors that have had a distorting effect, and to make corrective judgments." Yet if one were planning to contribute his services for laboratory ESP testing, he should submit to hypnosis if the parapsychologist he is working with suggests it. And so far, until we learn all those techniques of personal mind control, hypnosis is extremely useful therapeutically. As early as the First World War, German doctors used hypnosis as an anesthetic when medical supplies ran short, and British doctors reported its use to help shell-shocked soldiers recover their emotional balance. In the Second World War, scores of military doctors and psychiatrists testified to the value of hypnosis to stop bleeding, blank out pain, and restore minds disoriented by battle fatigue.

It is odd that not only does the mind obey the hypnotist, but it causes the body to do likewise. If ammonia is held under the subject's nose and he is told it is cologne, he smells it eagerly and his eyes do not water. When he smells cologne under the assumption that it is ammonia, he sneezes and his eyes produce a rain storm. If a pencil eraser is touched against the arm and the subject is told it is a hot iron, a blister will form there as from an actual burn.

And yet the stigmata of the saints comes from *self*-hypnosis of a similar sort. One who dwells on the wounds of Christ, desiring to see them exhibited on his own body, may discover that one day they have appeared, and they occur repeatedly after that, either at intervals or continuously.

It seems to me that the greatest challenge of hypnosis is in just such areas—learning to control the body by controlling the mind. The whole world would be a better place if each person knew how to keep himself healthy by his proper thinking. Of course, this is a long time in the future—but who is to say it might not eventually be accomplished?

There is so much we have to learn about how to use hypnosis. Many of our practitioners may be doing it all wrong, and there may be better ways to accomplish it than even the most successful at present suspect. Certainly there will be *different* ways.

"Look deep into my eyes . . ." may be the popular concept of how the hypnotist leads his subject into trance, but Dr. William Chapman has been proving otherwise for some twenty years. Recently retired, Chapman is the only blind hypnoanalyst known to the medical profession. He used hypnotism frequently in his practice at the outpatient clinic of the University of Virginia Hospital's Department of Psychiatry.

"People are generally easy to hypnotize, especially once they have experienced it," says Chapman, who amply compensates for, ignores, rarely mentions, and leads you to forget his blindness. "I can tell when they're asleep by listening to the breathing or feeling the pulse. Just a gentle touch on the arm is enough to tell."

Even the techniques of the mesmerists may have something from which we could learn, if we do not ignore them completely because they are old-fashioned and unsophisticated.

Without spending as much time, but with passes and stroking, perhaps such ways as this would be more successful in approaching those persons today who are supposed to be unhypnotizable. Your author is one of those who has never been able to cooperate fully with the techniques now used, although some of the best hypnotists in the country have tried to entrance me. I rather suspect that if someone showed me a flickering light or rotating colors such as the Russians are using I might go under. Or even mesmeric passes might seduce me. But when talked to, I listen too carefully. As a writer, I am one who deals with words constantly. I think of their sound and pronunciation and meaning. Thus when someone begins to tell me I am going to sleep, I pay attention closely to what he says and how he says it, and I find a slight tendency to edit, to criticize his pronunciation, to wonder why he is so repetitive, or why he is perhaps not more repetitive.

I do not have the ability to be able to produce mental pictures at will, and so when told to see pictures or to visualize myself in a certain place or situation, I find it impossible to do so. But I listen to the words carefully and agreeably— at first. I can always be brought to the initial stage, quite willing to follow all instructions, and when told I cannot open my eyes, I do not open them. I know it could be done if I really wanted to, but, being eager to cooperate, I don't want to. And my arm will rise into the air when it is told to.

Unfortunately, just about then the hypnotist will usually tell me to begin to visualize myself somewhere doing something, or he will tell me I am asleep when I know I am not, and I will begin mentally arguing with him. I do not mean to and do not want to; but that is my nature.

One night a professional hypnotist was invited to my home

in New York City to a psychic development group meeting, with the object that if he could hypnotize me, I might learn to go into a mediumistic trance. It was hoped that by having other members of the group present support would be lent to our endeavors.

I followed the operator's instructions perfectly as he began to talk eloquently and confidently: "You're getting sleepy . . . etc. On the count of ten your eyes will close and you will be unable to open them." I was with him all the way.

He went on: "Your right arm is rising slowly, slowly. It is so light it is floating in the air. You can't put it down. It rises right up to your nose and you lay your finger alongside your nose."

Still with him, I put my finger solidly alongside my nose. But then he went on: "Now you're swinging in a hammock."

"Why doesn't the darn fool get my finger down from my nose before he puts me in a hammock," I thought, alert, nonsleepy, eyes open, finger down from nose, sitting up, and slightly cranky about the whole thing. Who wants to be swinging in a hammock with his finger firmly clamped alongside his nose?

When they saw I was out of it, people across the room began to call out: "Look at Naomi!" And sure enough, suggestible Naomi's head was hanging on her chest and she was out—way out. She'd been listening to my treatment and taking it all in, and the idea of swinging in the hammock was just too much for her. She had swung right into a hypnotic state.

So there are different kinds of minds that react differently to hypnosis; and some people find it possible to perform all the feats of hypnotism while using their own minds instead of having someone else inflict his will on them. No matter how determined we are to think positively about the value of this force, it must be admitted, as Dr. Emilio Servadio said at the International Conference on Hypnosis, Drugs and Psi Induction at St. Paul-de-Vence, France, in 1967:

Hypnosis shows that a person in perfect physical and mental health can become the passive instrument of psychological forces that dominate him and that he cannot control. Hypnosis shows that hypnotic commands temporarily wipe out certain distinctions, such as those that separate reality and unreality, true and false—in brief, the very pivots of our lives, of our . . . psychical security. Through hypnosis man finds himself suddenly face to face with his innermost self which is at one and the same time powerful and irrational. . . . Hypnosis, however much one may try to limit and circumscribe it scientifically, contains elements that sooner or later tend to place the Ego in contact with disquieting and irrational aspects of the personality.

We have to remember also not to try to isolate hypnotism when we think about it. It is often presented as though it comprised a quite distinct group of phenomena. But instead, it is so intricately woven with all other aspects of life that it cannot be separated. Take today's television, even, constantly attempting to influence our thoughts about our buying habits and to mass hypnotize us into various beliefs. We hardly know where our own thoughts end and those of others impinging on us begin. Certainly it is something to be conscious of and concerned about.

It is in its uses in the wider area of our philosophical lives that hypnosis will probably end up being the most helpful to us. Allan Angoff pointed this out in his discussion of America's great philosopher and psychologist.

"But William James," he said, "went far beyond the therapeutic value of hypnosis. He studied it as a phenomenon which might yet give a cosmic view of the human psyche and the illimitable promise it held for future psychical research- ers."

Perhaps, if handled very carefully, yet developed open- mindedly and constructively, hypnosis holds illimitable promise for the future of us all.

Bibliography

Ambrose, Gordon and Newbold, George. *Hypnosis in Health and Sickness.* New York: John deGraff, Inc., 1958.

Angoff, Allan. "Hypnotism in the United States 1800–1900," *Abnormal Hypnotic Phenomena*, Vol. 4. Ed. Eric Dingwall. London: J. & A. Churchill, Ltd., 1968.

———. "The Literature of Hypnosis," *Tomorrow* (Autumn 1958).

Assailly, Alain. "Thoughts on Psychophysiological Components which May Play a Role in the Mediumistic State," *International Journal of Parapsychology*, Vol. 9, No. 2 (1967).

Barber, Theodore X. "Toward a Theory of 'Hypnotic' Behavior: The 'Hypnotically Induced Dream,'" *Journal of Nervous and Mental Disease*, Vol. 135 (1962).

Bekhterev, V. M. "Concerning Experiments on 'Thought' Influence on the Behavior of Animals," Questions of Personality Study and Education, No. 2 (1920).

Boirac, Émile. *Psychic Science.* London: William Rider & Son, 1918.

Braid, James. *Neurypnology: or the Rationale of Nervous Sleep.* London: J. S. Churchill, Ltd., 1843.

———. *Braid on Hypnotism.* New York: The Julian Press, Inc., 1960.

Caldwell, Charles. *Facts in Mesmerism and Thoughts on Its Causes and Uses*. Louisville, Ky., 1842. (No publisher)

Cannon, A. "Hypnosis in Criminology," *British Journal of Medical Hypnotism*, Vol. 1, No. 4 (Summer 1950).

Cayce, Edgar Evans. "Miracles were My Father's Business," *Fate* (May 1960).

Cerminara, Gina. *Many Mansions*. New York: William Sloane Associates, 1950.

Christenson, J. A., Jr. "Dynamics in Hypnotic Induction," *Experimental Hypnosis*. Ed. L. M. LeCron. New York: The Macmillan Co., 1952.

Coughlan, Robert. "Pathway into the Mind," *Life* (March 7, 1960).

Cuddon, Eric. *Hypnosis: Its Meaning and Practice*. London, 1955. (No publisher)

Davis, Andrew Jackson. *Divine Revelations*. New York: S. S. Lyon & William Fishbough, 1847.

Deleuze, F. *Histoire Critique de Magnétisme Animal*. Paris: Hippolyte Baillière, 1819.

De Rochas, Albert. *Les Vies Successives*. Paris, 1911. (No publisher)

Desmond, Shaw. *The Power of Faith Healing*. New York: Liveright Publishing Corp., 1957.

Dingwall, Eric J., ed. *Abnormal Hypnotic Phenomena*, Vol. 4. London: J. & A. Churchill, Ltd., 1968.

Ducasse, C. J. *A Critical Examination of the Belief in a Life After Death*. Springfield, Illinois: Charles C Thomas, 1961.

Durant, Charles F. *Exposition, or a New Theory of Animal Magnetism*. New York, 1837. (No publisher)

Ebon, Martin, ed. *Psychic Discoveries by the Russians*. New York: New American Library, 1971.

———. "Russia Explores 'Inner Space,'" *Tomorrow* (Winter 1962).

———. *They Knew the Unknown*. New York: The World Publishing Co., 1971.

Edmunds, Simeon. *Hypnotism and ESP*. Hollywood, Calif.: Wilshire Book Co., 1961.

Erle, R. A. "The Representation of Temporal Features of Events in Hypnotically Induced Dreams: An Exploratory Study." Master's thesis. Worcester, Mass.: Clark University, 1958.

Estabrooks, George H. *Hypnotism.* New York: E. P. Dutton, 1943.

Fahler, Jarl. "Does Hypnosis Increase Psychic Powers?" *Tomorrow* (Autumn 1958).

Flournoy, T. *From India to the Planet Mars.* Paris and Geneva, 1900. (No publisher)

Fodor, Nandor. "Three Women; One Body," *Tomorrow* (Autumn 1957).

Fontan, Professor (no first name). *Revue Philosophique,* August 1887. *Proceedings* Society for Psychical Research, Vol. 5.

Garrett, Eileen J. "Roads to Greater Reality," *Tomorrow* (Autumn 1958).

Gindes, Bernard C. *New Concepts of Hypnosis.* Hollywood, Calif.: Wilshire Book Co., 1968.

Glasner, Samuel. "Social Psychological Aspects of Hypnosis," *Hypnodynamic Psychology.* Ed. Milton V. Kline. New York: The Julian Press, Inc., 1955.

Gley, E. *Tribune Médicale.* May, 1875. (No publisher)

Gurney, Edmund. "Stages of Hypnotic Memory," *Proceedings* S.P.R., Vol. 2, No. 4.

Haddock, J. W. *Somnolism and Psycheism,* 2nd ed. London, 1851. (No publisher)

Hardinge, Emma. *Modern American Spiritualism: A Twenty Years' Record of the Communion Between Earth and the World of Spirits.* New York, 1870. (No publisher)

Honorton, Charles. "Significant Factors in Hypnotically-Induceu Clairvoyant Dreams," *Journal* A.S.P.R., Vol. 66, No. 1 (January 1972).

—— and J. P. Stump. "A Preliminary Study of Hypnotically-Induced Clairvoyant Dreams," *Journal* A.S.P.R., Vol. 63, (1969).

Huxley, Laura Archera. *The Timeless Moment.* New York: Ballantine, 1968.

James, William. "Report of the Committee on Mediumistic Phenomena." *Proceedings* A.S.P.R., Vol. 1 (1885–89).

Janet, Pierre and Gibert, Dr. (no first name). Bulletins de la So-
ciété de Psychologie, Tome I. *Revue Philosophique*. August
1886. (No publisher or city)

Johnson, Douglas. "The Mechanics of Mediumship." *Light* (Summer 1969).

Johnson, Richard F. "Hypnosis: What it Can and Can't Do for
You," *Science Digest*, Vol. 66, No. 3 (September 1969).

Kahn, David E. *My Life with Edgar Cayce*. Garden City, N.Y.:
Doubleday & Co., 1970.

Kahn, S. David. "Svengali Revisited," *Tomorrow* (Autumn 1958).

Kerner, Justinus. *The Seeress of Prevorst*. 1829. (No city or publisher)

Klein, D. B. "The Experimental Production of Dreams During
Hypnosis," University of Texas Bulletin #3009 (1930).

Kline, Milton V., ed. *Hypnodynamic Psychology*. New York: The
Julian Press, Inc., 1955.

LeCron, Leslie. "Hypnosis in the Production of Psi Phenomena,"
International Journal of Parapsychology (Summer 1961).

———. *Self-Hypnosis*. New York: Dell Publishing Co., 1971.

Levinson, Lee Edwards. "Hypnosis: The Key to Unlocking Latent
Psi Faculties," *International Journal of Parapsychology*
(Summer 1968).

Liepman, Heinz. *Rasputin, a New Judgement*. London: Frederick
Muller, Ltd., 1958.

Lobsenz, Norman M. "Hypnosis," *Good Housekeeping* (June
1969).

Ludwig, A. M. "Experiments at the Federal Narcotics Center in
Lexington, Ky." Report on the International Conference
"Hypnosis, Drugs, and Psi Induction," *Newsletter* of the
Parapsychology Foundation, Vol. 14, No. 4 (July–August,
1967).

Mazer, M. "An Experimental Study of the Hypnotic Dream,"
Psychiatry, Vol. 14 (1951).

Meerloo, Joost A. M. "Crime and Hypnosis," *Parapsychology Review* (March–April 1970).

Mitchell, Stanley V. "Can Hypnosis Break Through the Language
Barrier?" *Fate* (February 1963).

Moll, J. Albert. *Hypnotism*. London: Walter Scott, 1891.
——. *The Study of Hypnosis*. New York: The Julian Press, Inc., 1958.
Myers, F. W. H. *Human Personality and Its Survival of Bodily Death*. New Hyde Park, N.Y.: University Books, 1961.
—— and Dr. A. T. Myers. *Proceedings* S.P.R. Vol. 4.
O'Shaughnessy, Michael. "Andrew Jackson Davis—'Poughkeepsie Seer'," *Tomorrow* (Autumn 1960).
Ostrander, Sheila and Lynn Schroeder. *Psychic Discoveries Behind the Iron Curtain*. Englewood Cliffs, N.J.: Prentice-Hall, Inc., 1970.
Pagenstecher, Gustav. "Past Events Seership: A Study in Psychometry," *Proceedings* A.S.P.R., Vol. 16 (1922).
Podmore, Frank. *From Mesmer to Christian Science*. New Hyde Park, N.Y.: University Books, 1963.
Pratt, J. G., H. H. J. Keil, and Ian Stevenson. "Three-Experimenter ESP Tests of Pavel Stepanek During his 1968 Visit to Charlottesville," *Journal* A.S.P.R., Vol. 64, No. 1 (January 1970).
Prince, Morton. *Dissociation of a Personality*. London: Longmans, Green, 1930.
——. "Report to the International Congress of Psychology," *Proceedings* S.P.R., Vol. 15 (1921).
Prince, Walter Franklin. "Psychometric Experiments with Señora María Reyes de Z." *Proceedings* S.P.R. Vol. 15 (1921).
Roffenstein, G. "Experimentelle Symboltraeume: ein Beitrag zur Diskussion ueber Psychoanalyse." *Organization and Pathology of Thought*. New York: Columbia University Press, 1951.
Roll, W. G. "Pagenstecher's Contribution to Parapsychology," *Journal* A.S.P.R., Vol. 61, No. 3 (July 1967).
Rowland, L. W. "Will Hypnotized Persons Try to Harm Themselves or Others?" *Journal of Abnormal Social Psychology*, Vol. 34 (1939).
Ryzl, Milan. "A Method of Training in ESP," *International Journal of Parapsychology* (Autumn 1966).
——. *Parapsychology: A Scientific Approach*. New York: Hawthorne Press, 1970.

Schneider, Sidney A. "Report on Hypnotic Age Regression," *Fate* (October 1965).

Servadio, Emilio. "Hypnosis and Parapsychology: A Short Historical Survey," *Newsletter Parapsychology Foundation* (July–August 1967).

Sidis, Boris. *The Psychology of Suggestion*. New York: 1898.

Smith, Susy. *Out-of-Body-Experiences for the Millions*. Los Angeles: Sherbourne Press, 1968.

———. *Reincarnation for the Millions*. Los Angeles: Sherbourne Press, 1967.

———. *World of the Strange*. New York: Pyramid Books, 1963.

Spence, Lewis. *Encyclopedia of Occultism*. New Hyde Park, N.Y.: University Books, 1960.

Steiger, Brad. *The Psychic Feats of Olof Jonsson*. Englewood Cliffs, N.J.: Prentice-Hall, 1971.

Stevenson, Alwyn. "Hypnotizing by Telepathy," *Fate* (October 1960).

Stevenson, Florence. *A Feast of Eggshells*. New York: New American Library, 1970.

Sutcliffe, J. P. and Jean Jones. "Personal Identity, Multiple Personality, and Hypnosis," *The International Journal of Clinical and Experimental Hypnosis*, Vol. 10, No. 4 (October 1962).

Tart, Charles T. "The Control of Nocturnal Dreaming by Means of Posthypnotic Suggestion," *International Journal of Parapsychology* (Autumn 1967).

Thigpen, C. H. and H. M. Cleckley. *The Three Faces of Eve*. New York: McGraw-Hill, 1957.

Vassili, Leon. *Behind the Veil at the Russian Court*. London: Cassell & Co., Ltd., 1913.

Watkins, J. G. "Antisocial Compulsions Induced Under Hypnotic Trance," *Journal of Abnormal Social Psychology*, Vol. 42, (1947).

———. "A Case of Hypnotic Trance Induced in a Resistant Subject in Spite of Active Opposition," *British Journal of Medical Hypnosis*, Vol. 2, No. 4 (Summer 1951).

Wells, W. R. "Experiments in the Hypnotic Production of Crime," *Journal Psychology*, Vol. 11 (1941).

Williams, Loring G. "Reincarnation of a Civil War Victim," *Fate* (December 1966).

Wilson, Colin. *Rasputin and the Fall of the Romanovs.* New York: Farrar, Straus, 1964.

Wingfield, Hugh. "The Connection of Hypnotism with the Subjective Phenomena of Spiritualism," *Proceedings* S.P.R., Vol. 5.

Wirt, Edgar. "Dualism is with Us Again," *Spiritual Frontiers* (Winter 1972).

Index

Fahler, Jarl, 199–201
Fancher, Mollie, 150
Faraday cage, 216
"Fascination Method," 10
Fate magazine, 113, 126, 141, 190, 197
Federal Narcotics Center, 126
Field, George, 142
Finne, V.N., 215, 216
Fishbough, William, 69
Flournoy, T., 133
Flower, Sydney L., 72
Fludd, Robert, 17
Fodor, Nandor, 148, 149
Fontan, Professor, 46, 47
Foundation for Research on the Nature of Man, 212
Frankenstein, 86
Franklin, Benjamin, 22, 27, 64
From India to the Planet Mars (Flournoy), 133
From Mesmerism to Christian Science (Podmore), 22

Galen, 69
Ganushina Psychoneurological Clinic, 196
Garrett, Eileen J., 106–109
Gassner, J.J., 19–21, 24
Ghosts, 57, 59
Gibert, Dr., 47–50
Gindes, Bernard C., 1, 8, 9, 14, 23, 26, 158
Gladden, Lee, 223–227
Glasner, Samuel, 124, 160, 161
Gley, E., 51
Good Housekeeping, 6, 167
Great Harmonia, The (Fishbough), 69
Greatrakes, Valentine, 18, 19
Greenwood, Robin, 224–227
Gregory, William, 41
Grimes, J. Stanley, 68
Gurney, Edmund, 45, 120, 121

Haddock, J.W., 40, 56
Hands Across Space (Gladden and Williams), 223
Hardinge, Emma, 116–118
Hardrup, Pelle, 162, 163
Hartshorn, Thomas C., 65

Hauffe, Frederika, 57–60
Hawthorne, Nathaniel, 86
Hayakawa, S.I., 82
Health readings, 140
Honorton, Charles, 187, 190
Houston, Sam, 70
"How Hypnotism Saved Me" (Curtis), 2
Human Personality and Its Survival of Bodily Death (Myers), 48, 74
Huxley, Aldous, 181, 182
Hypnosis at a distance, 30, 48–53, 177–182, 216
"Hypnosis in Criminology" (Cannon), 159
Hypnosis in Health and Sickness (Ambrose and Newbold), 10
"Hypnosis in the Production of Psi Phenomena" (LeCron), 135, 180
Hypnosis: Its Meaning and Practice (Cuddon), 144
"Hypnosis: The Key to Unlocking Latent Psi Faculties" (Levinson), 11, 193
"Hypnosis: What it Can and Can't Do for You" (Johnson), 77
Hypnotic healer, 114
Hypnotism (Estabrooks), 173
Hypnotism (Moll), 160
Hypnotism and E.S.P. (Edmunds), 4, 163
"Hypnotism in the United States 1800–1900" (Angoff), 65
"Hypnotizing by Telepathy" (Stevenson), 190

Institute of Parapsychology, 203
Instruction pratique sur le Magnétisme Animal (Deleuze), 65
International Committee for Psychical Research, 214
International Conference on Hypnosis, Drugs, and Psi Induction, 237
International Journal of Parapsychology, 180, 186, 193, 205
Isis, 14

James, Horace, 118
James, William, 72, 237
Janet, Jules, 48
Janet, Paul, 48
Janet, Pierre, 32, 47, 48, 50, 190